911 – ¢OMMON-$ENSE MONEY

I BELIEVE I CAN THRIVE

Keith Ambersley

Published by Keith Ambersley, Marietta, GA

ISBN 13-978-0-615-29414-8

911 – COMMON SENSE MONEY

Contents

Foreword...7
Preface..9

Part 1

1   Whom Do I Thank for My Misery? 15

Part 2

2   911 – After Shock... 23
3   The Courage to Hope.. 29
4   The Gift that Keeps on Taking 39
5   Lose the Debt Not Your House 47
6   It's About the Money Stupid.. 55

Part 3

7   Mind Over Money.. 63
8   Think Positive! Be an Optimist.................................... 67
9   Recovery on the Rebound 71
10   911 – Cash Conservation 77
11   Ninety-One 911 Tips 83
12   Eye on Your Money 103
13   Squeeze the Money out of Foreclosure Costs 117
14   Make More Money from Compound Interest.............. 125
15   Repair Distressed Credit – Save $100s.............................. 133
16   Squeeze More Money from Car Loans
      and Warranties.. 139
17   The Common Sense in Banking 143
18   Squeeze the Cents from Your Taxes 147
19   Exercise Your Right to Negotiate Save $1,000s.................... 153
20   Thrive 163
21   The Bottom Line 171
22   A Word for Main Street 179
      Glossary of Terms 185

FOREWORD

"This time I'm gonna save for rainy days!" How many times have you heard (or even said) these words? Saving for a rainy day means deliberately reducing our daily, weekly, or monthly spending and depositing the leftover amount into a savings account or other reserve fund to be used only in case of a serious emergency.

Intuitively, we all know that we should do this. Our intellect tells us that if hard times find us without a nest egg, we and those who depend on us are likely to suffer significant and unpleasant consequences. Keith Ambersley is a family man who has lived in the United Kingdom and the West Indies. Keith also happens to work for one of the largest professional services companies in the world and one of the Big Four auditors. 911 – Common Sense Money is a simply written, "down to earth" book in which Ambersley quietly reminds us that only one out of every five Americans has actually prepared a reasonable family nest egg.

Believing that "it is better to light a candle than to curse the dark," Ambersley explains why we as Americans seldom prepare a family or personal nest egg. He reveals to us that wise saving is not painful. He shows us that wise saving is not only possible, but indeed, practical and even pleasant. Finally, the author systematically shows us how we can actually enjoy ourselves as we save for future "rainy days," which are certain to come either sooner or later.

Whether you are an intellectually curious business person, a serious-minded family member or even an "unattached" reader, you are likely to ask yourself, "Why didn't I discover this exciting and informative book before?" More importantly, as a college professor, I strongly recommend that the lessons of 911 – <u>Common Sense Money</u>, by Keith Ambersley, be taught to all college and even high school students before they encounter their inevitable "financial 911."

Charles L. Meadows, Ph.D., Director
Center for Teacher Preparation
Morehouse College

PREFACE

Times are tough, and saving money is on everyone's mind. 911 – Common Sense Money provides timely information and inspires hope beyond the worst economic crisis in more than 70 years. You will not find this information anywhere else.

This has been a year of dramatic change for our country and the economy. You are probably experiencing some kind of change in your own life, as well. Today, financial security is in the heart of every American. Building and strengthening your financial security is at the heart of this book.

Many will agree that this economic downturn has enabled millions of financially challenged Americans to think about smarter ways to manage their money. 911 – Common Sense Money enhances this thinking, as households gravitate more towards the lean side of spending. My book goes beyond living on emergency funds. It provides hope and a recovery plan. You will discover that there are so many 911 Tips you have never thought about. This book brings them to your attention. Take the 911 – Common Sense Money challenge. It's practical, achievable, straightforward, and simple (PASS) it on.

The U.S. Department of Labor reports that four million men and women between the ages of 33–48 also known as the Generation X (Gen X) are now unemployed because of this economic downturn. Who are these four million men and women? They are family members, friends, and acquaintances. These are the men and women who pay taxes, own homes, and contribute to the U.S. economy.

Until now, the Gen X population has never experienced a crisis like this in their lifetime. Insecurity and stress is fast becoming a 911 cry for help. The path of excess enjoyed several years ago by this generation now seems like a million miles away.

Four million Americans hope to emerge from this crisis stronger and more determined to succeed. This is possible even against a backdrop of increasing unemployment, and home foreclosures.

How to reduce personal expenses, build financial security, and thrive during this economic downturn is a major component of this book. Recovery starts in the mind, not the pocket. The choice is simple! What should go first? Some consumers find this exercise easier to accept than others do. 911 – Common Sense Money targets the attitude about managing money. It identifies common problems and provides common sense answers.

Jane is a 40-year-old Gen X mother and wife. This is her story. Jane started working in corporate America fifteen years ago. Jane worked her way from the bottom to a senior position, putting in sixty-hour workweeks. Jane has been through a couple of economic downturns but nothing to this extreme. Today, Jane has a family to support and no job.

Jane is one of four million displaced by this economic downturn. Despite the <u>deep impact</u> that this recession is having on household income, Jane has two things going for her: she has the will to survive and the drive to thrive.

This book is the <u>road map</u> to help financially challenged individuals and families like Jane discover hope in these difficult times. 911 – Common Sense Money is about highlighting practical and relevant everyday tips that work. This book is a gut-check guide which revives the time-tested **<u>no frills</u>** money management strategy for a tough economy. 911 – Common Sense Money is part information, motivation, and inspiration. It provides the financial tools for Jane and you to <u>thrive.</u>

PART
<u>1</u>

1

WHOM DO I THANK FOR MY MISERY?

You've probably heard this said so many times: "The Devil is in the details." The most fluent and well informed reader can miss important information buried in the details of a contract. You may have applied for a car loan or home mortgage and in the process you were handed a twenty-page document to review and sign in five minutes. That's a lot of pressure! Ninety percent (90%) of readers don't remember key details contained in those twenty pages. Furthermore, they do not ask the relevant questions that help them understand the terms of the agreement. This is a common mistake.

A loan officer tells you the payment for the first three years will be 4%. There will be incremental increases of half percent (.5%) in year four up to a maximum 7%. In your mind, you heard 4%. This is what you have planned for. To you the 7% is irrelevant because it's not current. Suddenly, 4% sounds like a great offer until the fourth year, when your payments increase and you have to come up with extra cash that was not part of your budget.

The credit card company sends you a statement, and buried in the details is a clause that says if you miss one payment, your interest will increase by 10%. These are common mistakes that are overlooked and end up causing so much misery.

It is easy to look for someone or something to blame. Never accept money without taking time to read and understand the fine-print. This is a major cause for financial hardships. What you don't know can really hurt you. The evidence is clear as millions try to secure a family safety net after being burned by the credit and housing meltdown.

Errors in judgment are a common mistake, especially when there is a misunderstanding of the facts. We say to ourselves, this will never happen again! Details are missed when we are under pressure. In this age of instant everything; be careful and know exactly what you are committing yourself to.

There is no quick-fix method to correct these mistakes. Over a period of time these mistakes become unmanageable if left unattended. Serious-minded consumers know that a solution is effective only if you have identified the problem. In other words, a band-aid is not recommended for a headache.

The days of subprime lending that allowed consumers to go beyond their ability to repay debt are over. There is an overwhelming consumer sentiment for a return to "simple, old-fashioned lending, and money management values." A common sense approach to managing money is required to lead Americans out of this abyss of foreclosures and rising debt. Past financial mistakes can be corrected. Taking the common sense approach is a great place to start.

A year ago, saving for the "rainy day" was the last thing on most consumers' minds. Today, Americans are getting back to the basics of conservative spending and saving over consumerism. This current economic climate continues to remind men and women of this great country of a timeless value forgotten: Every penny counts. A new way of thinking is emerging, which goes beyond consumerism.

The "spend it all now" approach to money management is now replaced with a conservative view. Greater financial security and stability will result from this new wave of common sense thinking. The stage is being set for a major financial comeback.

This financial crisis gives us valuable insight regarding the broad impact caused by money mismanagement. It makes sense that sacrifice and hard work is required to get us through this tough period. Activating personal money management applications will in the end put those currently at risk back on the road to financial recovery.

The Wright brothers used common sense to make aviation history by creating a method called "Wing warping" (a revolutionary system was designed by twisting an empty bicycle tube box with the ends removed). By twisting the surface of each 'wing,' it changed the position in relation to oncoming wind. Such changes in position would result in changes in the direction of flight. Wilbur Wright tested his theory using a small kite, and it worked.

The U.S. economy is taking a big hit as jobs are lost, investments are shrinking, and housing finds itself in a spiraling "nosedive." To prevent one becoming another financial casualty, one has to **pull up** on excess spending and reduce debt.

The "reset button" has been engaged on the economy and our lives. What does the future hold for Jane and the four million unemployed— men and women financially displaced by this economic downturn? Recovery from the bottom is going to be hard work. With determination and common sense, those Americans that have made sacrifices through this downturn will have their dream. It's not about being "cheap"; it's about being smart! Working to correct yesterday's problems today lays the foundation for a brighter tomorrow. If you don't see it, just believe it.

American families like Jane are taking advantage of this once-in-a-lifetime opportunity to adjust current lifestyles in a meaningful way. It's all about security in these challenging times and beyond. Becoming leaner in one's finances increases the chance to thrive and reduce stress. The opportunities brought about by an economic downturn are a terrible thing to waste. Benefit from every experience, and make it count for something. One of the benefits provided by 911 – Common Sense Money is that it takes the confusing elements out of money management by providing real life examples for the regular person with average to mediocre credit and financial bandwidth.

On **Main Street**, consumers have very little money to spend. We are all working with less. There is just not enough cash to go around. This is happening against a backdrop of job losses, home foreclosures and the increasing burden of personal debt. Main Street consumers are trying to cut a little fat off everything. Most are running into roadblocks and are getting frustrated in the process. It took time to get in and it will take time to get out of debt. An achievable financial goal should include using common sense to strike a balance between being leaner with spending and living a comfortable life during this cash crisis.

Jane and four million unemployed men and women just want a way out. Jane's biggest fear is that the next series of Subprime to Prime market-driven events appear to be on the horizon. The longer this crisis continues the more likely even folk with good credit will be at risk. 911 – Common Sense Money helps you to be proactive and reduce that risk.

Jane has the power to make the best choices available to manage her money even with limited options at her disposal.

For many Americans they are facing a red sea of debt, mountains of foreclosure on both sides and the economic forces of unemployment closing in on Main Street consumers. The key is to focus on the outcome. Create a plan and see it through. Believe that you can, and you will thrive through this.

On **Wall Street**, Corporations continue to face challenges to raise cash for production on one hand and declining revenues on the other. The financial market continues to feel the slack of consumer and business confidence. Bank lending is still in a state of flux and unemployment concerns are at an all time high. On the one hand, banks and financial institutions have restricted lending to Main Street consumers and businesses. On the other hand, after being bailed out themselves, banks are hoarding money with the intent to make their bottom line financials look good which also creates the illusion of recovery. This is all happening while American families and the economy struggle to thrive. Moreover, many state and local governments are facing fiscal pressure. Cutting costs and creating additional ways to tax residents who are already struggling appears to be the "new normal."

The U.S. sneezed and the rest of the world is getting a cold. There are many fingers pointing to the U.S. as the source of everyone's misfortune. However, all that negative energy needs to be channeled back to find solutions and develop ideas for recovery. When all the tiresome debates are over, we still need to get beyond this downturn. Lest we forget—everyone enjoyed the benefits of a boom economy which fueled consumption and excess.

As the recession kicks into high gear, consumers are feeling the pain. Is there going to be a bailout for millions of struggling American families? Yes there will be, but not in the form that you are looking for. You may be disappointed. The only sure thing is how well you take care of your money. Everything that comes after that is a benefit. **You have control over what you can control.**

You may be concerned that your retirement and investment fund continues to decline in value. Don't be anxious to sell. The stock markets are rebounding while the way is being paved for you to return to your pre-recession investment value. This is good news. The alternative is fear, resulting in withdrawal and financial defeat. Given time, your investments will thrive again.

The lesson learned from this crisis is that it's important to hold your broker and financial adviser more accountable for sharing timely information with you. This crisis has given investors invaluable insight into the brokerage world. It's so easy to sell when things are going well. To provide relevant and timely advice in a crisis when it really counts is just as critical.

Wall Street needs a vibrant Main Street. With the current rally in the stock market, Main Street continues to spend less and save more. This is done for self preservation and financial security. One smart bank has caught on by educating consumers to save through spending.

PART
<u>2</u>

2

911 – AFTER SHOCK

Many are celebrating the end of the recession, which is great. However, American families and individuals like Jane are still feeling the aftershocks right now and possibly into the future. The repair needed to invigorate stability is going to get easier as Americans take the disciplined approach to spending and saving more seriously. Home values continue to show the effects of the recession aftershock. Residential real estate prices have decreased by thirty percent in some areas of the country. Americans are paying for homes that if they were to go on the market, money would still be owed after the sale. Landlords in the commercial real estate world are struggling to pay for space that is empty, or the revenue stream has decreased to keep current tenants.

Families have nowhere to turn for help and others are on the verge of being homeless. What lesson can we learn from these events? Consumerism based on debt is not sustainable. There is no need at this point to be anxious about quick fixes. It is more important to be cautious about identifying the problem then deciding which solutions need to be applied.

Struggling families like Jane across America must replace fear with optimism. Recovery starts in the mind not in the pocket. Americans at risk have made many adjustments. However, there are creative ways to do more. The idea is to cushion the financial impact from the aftershock. Help and information like 911 – Common Sense Money is available. Always remember—you are not alone! You have control over what you can control.

Working Americans, too, need to scale back on excess spending, and operate on a tighter budget. There is no crystal ball to determine what will take place in your job or current finances. Therefore, even if you have enough now, spending only on what you need is a step in the right direction. Save the rest for the rainy day, this could be today.

The aftershock from this recession has affected the nest egg once held sacred by retired and retiring Americans. Retirees are coming back into the workforce to make ends meet. The aftershock continues even into retirement.

Consumers are confused about what they need to do to protect their families' financial security. What are the quick fixes? There is no quick fix, only <u>common sense</u>. Consider the current economy as the prospect of losing one's job increases. We see an alarming reverse in the American way of life. Everyone is either affected or at risk.

It does not matter if you have enough money or not. The rich are feeling the aftershock just like everyone else. There are countless stories of people with money who are actively working to limit the aftershock on their family security and wellbeing.

Unprecedented is a word reserved for an event that has no historic comparison. *Unprecedented* is an understatement when looking at the magnitude of the changes and disruptions to retirement funds, home values, families, communities and the nation.

I get questions like "my finances are a mess. what do you suggest I do?" I would look for areas where you are most vulnerable, and cut the financial excess over here to stop the bleeding expense over there. If there is nothing left to cut, negotiate with your creditor(s) by highlighting your good faith effort to pay.

Aftershocks cannot be prevented. However, by making adjustments and being smart with your money, you can limit the impact.

Now is the time to get busy on your recovery plan. The longer you wait to execute your plan, the longer your recovery will take. At the end of the day you want to live a decent life now and a better life when this is all over. Do whatever it takes for you and your family to work through the aftershock. This is a team effort.

Success is dependent on contributions from every member of the family. This financial mess is bigger than one person. Therefore, the family unit is responsible for the welfare and recovery of itself. This crisis should bring out the natural survival instinct in the family members. Be creative, make it fun!

An eight-year-old was recently interviewed about the effects of this recession and his money. The young man said he gets a $3 allowance. He spends half now on what he needs and saves the other half. He was asked, "Why not spend it all now?" The eight-year-old said he has goals for the other half. He does not intend to give up his goals!

Millions of Americans like Jane contemplate pulling money out of retirement funds to pay bills. This may be the "new normal" for individuals and families to sacrifice long-term plans for short-term relief. It is all about feeling secure. Like Jane, the average American family is tapping all available options. Jane's attitude is reflective of the mood across the nation. Jane, like millions of Americans, is not willing to sit by and do nothing. **Inaction is not an option neither is it acceptable.**

A Hewitt Associates survey found that 6.2 percent of retirement account participants' at large corporations had taken an early withdrawal as of September 30, compared with 5.1 percent who reported taking early withdrawals in 2006.

A separate October survey by the American Association of Retired Persons found that 13 percent of Americans 45 and older had tapped into their retirement investments early. The decision to dip into retirement funds early usually requires paying a heavy financial penalty. Experts warn of lost savings and the lost chance for interest income down the line. This has an impact on your tax and accounting position. You really want this to be a "last resort," said David Certner, legislative policy director for the AARP.

Now is the time for American families to <u>huddle down</u> and protect what is left of their finances. Work together as one unit with a common goal. Save as much as you can. Buying cheap is a survival tactic that fits the times. Get all the free help that you can. When things were better you gave to food banks, thrift stores, and the Salvation Army. Now that things have changed and you face your aftershocks, it's time to go and "get yours!"

A man was swimming in a lake and suddenly he had difficulty and went under water. He managed to come up and said in a soft tone, "Assistance please!" Under he went and came up again making the same soft plea, "Assistance please!" The third time under and coming up, he shouted, "HELP." Everyone cried out, "You should have said that before." This is not the time to be ashamed to ask for help and guidance, if you need it.

At this point, everyone is vulnerable and needs to take advantage of free advice and help. Collect all the vouchers in those marketing brochures that under better circumstances would end up in the trash.

Jane discovers there is hope in-spite of her financial aftershocks. These are uncertain times filled with hope for the future. Be encouraged. "The sun still shines behind the cloud."

Jane does not need a crystal ball for insight on the future. The future is dependent on the actions taken today. Reducing debt corrects yesterday's problems. This is a step in the right direction. With a little help, you hold the key to your own recovery.

This is the time when all Americans must pull together and look out for our neighbors. Survival should not be a catalyst to serve ourselves and forget everyone else. We are all in the trench together.

There are few job options in this tight economy. However, service jobs are available if you are not picky! I have worked on resumes that have enabled friends to find jobs in this market. The key is to stay engaged until things get better. Relocation may be an option for some who don't mind uprooting. Other folk are shaving the excess and living within their means. There is also the option to get involved in the community. Helping others is a great way to cope with this downturn.

Drastic times call for drastic measures. Corporations are a great example of what needs to be done to cope with the financial aftershocks. It's all about being lean, not mean. Common Sense tells you that you need to scale back and stop the bleeding expense. The key is to manage expenses wisely and adjust your lifestyle up and downward as the need arises.

Over a two-year period, I have surveyed college students, corporate associates, family and friends on debt issues. The students in particular have one common theme on the topic of **getting out of debt.** There is so much information available about managing debt. Why is the rate of personal debt still on the increase? The answer is just as simple as the question. Short term financial goals without common sense will not resolve long-term problems.

In the search for answers 911 – Common Sense Money is a practical and easy to apply guide for financial freedom. Common sense money targets the attitude about managing money and helps to change the thinking that drives compulsive spending. Consider tackling one or two small debts first to give you the psychological boost you need to keep going.

The federal stimulus is only part of your total recovery plan. The rest of the recovery is on you. You must find a way to take ownership and manage your finances. 911 – Common Sense Money is designed to empower you with ideas and examples to manage your finances in a practical way. **You have power over what you can control.**

Many organizations promise an array of instant recovery ideas to fix your financial problems. Don't get sucked in! These quick fixes are shallow; they are not even a viable alternative. Most quick fixes only mask and extend the problem. Common Sense needs to be engaged before requesting help from these organizations.

3

THE COURAGE TO HOPE

Hope is being challenged across America. Many families are going through the ultimate test as they encounter the financial pressures to put food on the table, pay the bills, and have a sense of financial security. It takes pure courage to hope under those kinds of pressures. The inadequacies of feeling like a failure are disturbing and real. Money issues have taken center stage in our lives.

The courage to hope increases as you thrive through this downturn. Hope takes the higher ground. "Just getting through it" is not good enough. Hope requires one to look forward with confidence and great expectation. Hope should not be an excuse to sit there and do nothing. Hope is action in motion. It's very important to "grease the wheels that drive the cart."

"Optimism is the faith that leads to achievement. Nothing can be done without hope and confidence."

HelenKeller.http://www.beyondthequote.com/helen-keller-quotes.html (accessed September 11, 2009).

No one hopes for what already exists. Finding the courage to hope in adversity is not an easy task. Hope believes and is not easily discouraged. Stay with me as we take a walk down Hope Street.

Hope is stronger and deeper than any economic challenge you may ever face. Hope is like a buoy. No matter how the sea rages, the buoy is still on top. Unwavering hope and hard work will give you the power to correct past mistakes, move forward, and thrive. If you believe this, recovery is on its way.

This economic problem goes beyond our worst expectation. However, if you feel helpless, don't quit on hope. Remember, someone is depending on you! For many Americans, hope is all they have left.

This economic downturn has infiltrated every aspect of commercial and social life in America. It affects cab drivers, the elderly, deli stores, insurance companies—and the list goes on. There is just not enough money to eat and play for now. Economists confirm that we are coming out of a two-year recession. When will this madness end? No one has a clue even though there is talk about "green shoots appearing."

There are so many fundamentals at play right now. The vital signs are very unsettling for Main Street consumers, as the insecurity of unemployment lurks in the shadow. We know the stock market is up; however, the writing is still on the wall. We are not out of the woods. There is just not enough consumer power to drive growth off the ground, much less to take it through the stratosphere. Consumers are the driving force behind economic growth and recovery. They are the first to go into the fire and the last to come out. If history is accurate, we are on the verge of something great. Common sense will tell you that you need to be prepared for it, spiritually, emotionally, and financially.

Right now, consumers are doing the right thing. They are gathering the courage to be smart with their money by spending less, paying down debt, and saving more. For now, this is the only way.

The following is representative of "What's up and down" with the U.S. economy:

1. Gasoline prices are lower than $4 saving you money at the pump.
2. Investors with any money left are pumping it into CDs, Bonds and gold.
3. America spends 75% of its GDP.
4. China, Singapore, and Australia spend 35% of their GDP.
5. Americans save more to have a cushion against future emergencies.
6. The war on personal and national debt continues.
7. Gold is up—if you can afford to buy it.
8. Utility prices are lower. May require shopping for rates prior to contract renewal.
9. The playing field between the rich and the poor is being leveled.
10. Sixty percent (60%) of the 700 billion dollar bailout is still not appropriated. Jane and other American families still hope to benefit from this.
11. Americans confidence is flat because of this downturn in the economy.
12. Cash and debt problems among consumers continue to rise.
13. Plenty of sales and deals are on Main Street.
14. Hard-hit banks have implemented stricter lending criteria with twenty percent (20%) down payments becoming the norm to borrow money.
15. The housing market will stay in decline with hopes to recover before the end of 2012.
16. Bargains in the housing market abound.
17. Everyone is fighting to survive and thrive.
18. Banks forced to discontinue improper overdraft billing practices.
19. American consumers become conscious about staying on the lean side of living.

In his most recent testimony, Alan Greenspan, former Federal Reserve Chairman, blamed the problems on heavy demand for securities backed by subprime mortgages by investors who did not worry that the boom in home prices might come to a crashing halt.

"Given the financial damage to date, I cannot see how we can avoid a significant rise in layoffs and unemployment," Greenspan said. "Fearful American households are attempting to adjust, as best they can, to a rapid contraction in credit availability, threats to retirement funds and increased job insecurity."

Greenspan said that a necessary condition for the crisis to end will be stabilization in home prices but he said that was not likely to occur for "many months in the future."

The Republican Newsroom Thursday October 23, 2008

http://www.masslive.com/news/index.ssf/2008/10/former_federal_reserve_chairma.html

---

The economic power of capitalism has experienced some serious setbacks. This is definitely a cool-off period to reset and reassess before we move forward. The future demands common sense, not more of the same actions that put us here in the first place.

This economic problem is a worldwide phenomenon. The world has become a woven network of transactions. Whatever we do in America affects the rest of the world. This is a result of our influence, size, and the ability to consume. Unemployed and debt-burdened consumers like Jane are fighting back to be more financially responsible. Jane may be down but not out. Gut check! It's important to hope for the strongest and most stable years of financial growth to come.

What will the history books say about this generation and how we handled this economic challenge? It should say that we were resilient and we thrived. We overcame one of the greatest financial challenges of our time through hope, courage and hard work.

Why do non-Americans assume that Americans carry a higher than average debt burden than anyone else in the developed world? This is not true, as our British friends are also deeply in debt. The average household debt in England stands at more than $100,000 per family, according to the charitable organization Credit Action.

Credit Action is a nationally established British money education charity that helps those that are financially vulnerable. These are big numbers with significant consequences. Two hundred and seventy five people are declared insolvent every day, equaling one insolvency every 4.8 minutes, the charity says.

Many Europeans are nervous due to this souring economic decline. Take Helen Mabberley, a 30-year-old, who has to refinance the mortgage on the one-bedroom apartment she bought four years ago. Helen estimates that she will end up paying $323 more a month on her mortgage. Like so many others, she feels like the situation is out of her control. "I literally don't understand what's going on," she said.

F. Brinley Bruton msnbc.com updated 8:00 p.m. ET, Wed., Oct. 22, 2008 http://www.msnbc.msn.com

In its monthly assessment of lending conditions, the British Bankers' Association stated that the amount of money outstanding on credit cards dropped by $484 million in December, while bank customers continued to pay off more of their overdrafts and personal loans than they took on. Outstanding debt dropped $301 million the fifth straight monthly fall. This is an indication that the level of personal debt in Britain is falling.

Times are tough for Jane as a consumer, mother and unemployed worker. However, the REAL American spirit shines brighter when the going gets tough. Americans, like Jane, never back down or give into the pressures of defeat. This is not arrogance. It's just who we are. America has been down this road before, and she rose to the challenge to become the world financial and technological powerhouse. To be precise, it was seventy-six years ago. Americans rode through the depression then, and we will triumph over all the challenging headwinds as they come upon us. In the famous words of Dr. Martin Luther King, Jr., "**We shall overcome**."

The tide is turning in favor of the American consumer when it comes to lower cost for items sold on Main Street. There is a 360-degree change in the attitude displayed by sellers towards consumers like Jane. We have to thank a bad economy for this change in behavior.

Right now many business owners are hurting, and they need every dollar they can put their hands on. During this economic challenging time, the seller is more than willing to listen and act in the consumer's best interest. This change in attitude represents a **Transfer of Power** from the seller to the consumer. The good news is that there is an opportunity to save more money in the process. Prices for clothing, food and gasoline continue to fall. There are strong signs of stronger price competition for these basic consumer items. If this were not so, we would really have something to complain about.

What does this transfer of power do for Jane and family? It costs less for essential commodities and services. The good news is that Jane now finds some relief as prices on food and other essentials are on an endless sale. Putting it in perspective, the cup is half-full.

As an example, the telephone company is charging ridiculous rates for servicing basic calls. Under the current economic conditions, with a little market competition, telephone companies will practically give you whatever you want to keep your business. Transfer of power has taken place. Remember, this is a buyer's market.

When the seller has the power, there is a negative effect on the consumer through higher prices, and lower customer service. Because of the current crisis, customer service has never been better. Thanks to the current economic downturn, Jane has the power to make practical financial changes supported by lower costs. If you pay less for essentials, it makes sense to save the savings and reduce debt.

Money matters. When something matters you take care of it. Jane and four million unemployed American men and women must continue to be smarter with their money. It is important to have tighter controls and stop the bleeding on all expenses. Lean, not mean, strikes the correct balance. 911 – Common Sense Money highlights that balance for the casual and serious-minded readers. This model helps to create the long-term financial security you need.

Hope springs out of chaotic situations. Excess spending was acceptable just a couple of years ago. Today it is not cool neither is it acceptable by most people's standards. Spend-thrift behaviors belong to a closed era. This is a new day and a new era. The greatest change that one can make is to become a true **21st century money manager** in your own way.

Many believe that **tomorrow will take care of it-self.** Tomorrow will take care of only those that have made their best preparation for it today.

In the middle of this downturn, many Americans still have a job. The current mindset of the American consumer is to save more and live on the lean side of spending. Saving for the rainy day has arrived for many, and for others, they hope for the best. The glass is half-full for many. Let's be thankful—things could be much different. Try empty! The temptation is always there to spend. If you don't need it, why buy it? Improving your financial security and reducing the stress and worry about money should be your goal.

Prior to two thousand and eight (2008), Jane was the beneficiary of the nation's stronger economic cycle of prosperity. As a nation built on the free market philosophy, we relish in the fact that capitalism has provided a better life to millions. Unfortunately, there is a dark side and we are now in it. The reality is that it's harder to get credit and find a job. This is an everyday occurrence. Jane understands that her **attitude is important**. Therefore, her outlook for the future is based on hope for a great recovery.

Unemployment and being on the verge of losing a home and income feels like the end of the world as it becomes harder to see the light at the end of the tunnel. For Jane and four million financially challenged Americans, this downturn is a reverse opportunity, not the end. **It's only a matter of perspective, which separates hope from defeat**. The idea is to see this as a new beginning, a type of cleansing. Many individuals and families have the desire to move beyond being victims of money misfortunes but lack the tools, will-power and the discipline to do anything about it. What should you do when there is a loss of financial control? It takes a little hope, will-power and redirection to ignite motivation. This economic downturn is the catalyst that is motivating consumers to bring everything back in focus. **You have control over what you can control.**

4

THE GIFT THAT KEEPS ON TAKING

Everyone views credit cards as a gift. This gift provides an easy way to buy now and pay whenever. Credit cards are a gift that just "keeps on taking." Credit cards take away the ability for you to save, live debt-free, and enjoy life on your terms.

Credit is meant to be a short-term convenience, not a lifestyle. This is why it is considered a loan if held for more than ninety (90) days. We are all encouraged to establish credit. However, over time, loosely managed credit and the ease of getting more credit make it possible for consumers to get in over their head. Uncontrolled interest payments can reduce your financial security and the ability to thrive for the rest of your life.

When there is any type of financial arrangement, the status is determined as either a loan or credit. Credit is designed to help as a payment bridge for 30 days. This is short term only. Loans are long term extending beyond 90 days.

The democratization of credit has really generated a competitive spending culture, and plastic has allowed for early access to consumer items not had by the previous generation. Most of us grew up in an age when cash was the in thing. Buying with cash helped us to control the urge to splurge. If you had no cash, there was no need to go shopping, for things we did not really need or could not afford.

The following represent the distinction between credit and a loan:

Credit
1. Credit guaranteed by a third party
2. Payment due after invoice processed
3. No interest charged on zero balance
4. No administrative fee
5. Guaranteed balance for emergencies
6. Interest "Compounded daily" on recurring balance
7. Interest on interest for late payments
8. Short-term bridge
9. Credit has no end date

Loan
1. Interest on interest for late payments
2. Penalties for late payment
3. Fixed or variable Interest based on the time value of money
4. Balances expected to be held for terms longer than ninety (90) days
5. Loan guaranteed by third party
6. Long term obligation
7. Loan has an end date

We need to get back to the original purpose for having credit. Let's face it—if you buy now and do not pay in thirty days, no credit card company is going to complain about you paying more for something that should have cost you less. When short-term credit becomes a long-term obligation, you have just crossed that line from credit to a hybrid loan. Revolving interest charges have no limit on a hybrid loan. There is a penalty you pay for using something long term that is intended to be short term only.

Credit used for such items as food, clothing, and other consumer goods should not be on your account beyond thirty days. If the credit balances for these purchases remains on your card for more than ninety days, this defeats the true purpose for using credit. Ninety days is stretching it.

It's cheaper to get a loan for a fixed amount and term than to have extended credit beyond 90 days. Compound interest over time wipes away any future saving opportunity that you would have had. Consumers need to realize that the interest rates charged on extended credit is 300% higher than a basic loan arrangement which at a maximum may be 8%. Consumers continue to feel the pressure caused by the revolving credit crunch. Credit impacts your future financial security, as you are forced to spend tomorrow's savings to cover today's expense. Take the common sense challenge. Is it cheaper to have a loan or credit? You decide!

In many cases the interest owed over time exceeds the money borrowed. No matter how many minimum payments you make, the account is never satisfied. This is what the gift of credit does to individuals and families if not managed properly. The only way out is to get out!

Consumers are returning the keys to their homes every day. You can not give back the card and think that it's over. You need to have a plan to negotiate or pay the balance down. Consumers need to take the disciplined approach to credit. Having ten cards per family is the only conceivable option for some. Scaling back is the other available option for others. Credit has become the bottomless pit for many American families. Every unpaid purchase increases the pressure and stress brought about by unresolved credit balances.

There is no real financial future if you forever owe the credit card company. All that exists is a mountain of debt that you must overcome for the rest of your natural life. You deserve better, and you're going to get it at the end of this book.

Cash is great! When I buy an item there is a mechanism of control with me and my money. Credit takes away any Conscious effort of control.

Here are some interesting statistics from an article titled, "Don't Get Clobbered by Credit Cards" by author and journalist, Gary Weiss:

The average American household's credit card debt in 1990 was **$2,966**. In 2007, it was **$9,840**. **60%** of U.S. consumers always (or usually) pay off their bills in full each month. The **40%** who don't pay off their bills each month are called "revolvers." In 2007, revolvers paid **$18.1 billion** in penalty fees to credit card companies. This figure is up more than **50%** since 2003 and accounts for approximately half of the industry's **$40.7 billion** in profits.

GaryWeissblog.http://www.parade.comandgaryweiss.blogspot.com/. (accessed December 22, 2008).

According to a study released by Bank rate, Inc. in February 2008:

In one survey **66%** of Americans say debt is often the result of unfortunate circumstances beyond a person's control, while in another survey **60%** say it is usually the result of bad decisions. Americans have conflicting attitudes about debt. While **91%** believe debt can be controlled by disciplined saving and spending, **72%** also believe that debt is a part of modern life and difficult to avoid.

Not true, uncontrolled spending is an addiction, not part of modern life! **Sixty four percent** of the people polled who carry debt admitted that debt is a cause of worry for them. The study found that men worry less than women do about debt.

Bankrate, Inc. http://www.bankrate.com

In **October 2007**, credit card debt that was at least **30 days late** totaled **$17.6 billion**, up **26%** from **October 2006**. Some credit card companies, including Advanta, GE Money Bank and HSBC, are reporting a **50% increase** in accounts that are at least **90 days late** compared to the same time last year.

MarkBrinker.http://www.hoffmanbrinker.com/credit-card-debt-statistics.html (accessed December 12, 2008).

The average college debt for recent graduates is more than $18,000 and rising.

Georgetown published information on the use of credit cards by college students. Statistics from that study show:

- College students carried an average of $552 in credit card debt, while young adults in the same age brackets carried an average balance of $1,465 on their credit cards.
- The average amount of credit extended to students was $1,395, which was considerably less than the $3,581 in credit obtained by young adults (non-students) of the same age. The average adult was able to obtain nearly $7,500 in credit.
- College students are more likely to pay off their credit card balance than any other demographic group studied.
- Moreover, while students are much more likely to pay off their balances, they tend to pay late and exceed their credit limits more frequently than other groups and therefore incur more fees than other groups.

The median credit card debt of low- and middle-income people aged 18 to 34 is $8,200.

Current statistics on debt gathered by this U.S. government agency include:

The size of the total consumer debt grew nearly five times in size from 1980 ($355 billion) to 2001 ($1.7 trillion). Consumer debt in 2008 now stands at $2.6 trillion.

People between the ages of 25 and 34 make up 22.7% of all U.S. bankruptcies (but just 14% of the population at large), according to a recent report. The current financial crisis has doubled and even quadrupled.

The average household in 2008 carried nearly $8,700 in credit card debt. As of the twelve months ending June 2006, there were 1.5 million consumer bankruptcy filings, including 1.1 million Chapter 7 filings, 0.1 million filings for Chapter 11 and 0.3 million Chapter 13 bankruptcies.

These same Americans own approximately 1.4 billion cards—an average of nearly nine credit cards issued per credit card holder.

In addition, Americans charged approximately $2,052 billion dollars to their credit cards in 2005—that is just over $12,500 in charges each year per cardholder. This information includes all credit card types including bankcards, phone cards, as well as credit cards issued by oil companies and retail store.

Finally, this data tells us that Americans carried approximately 832 billion dollars in credit card debt and that number will grow to a projected 1,091 billion dollars by the year 2010.

This works out to approximately $5,000 in credit card debt per cardholder (not household as mentioned in the Federal Reserve statistics mentioned earlier). Moreover, that number is expected to increase to nearly $6,200 by 2010.

Card companies continue to raise the interest rates on their customers. This is a total disregard for those hardworking account holders who have kept their side of the bargain. With that in mind, now is the time to exchange the gift that keeps on taking for the gift of independence. Put your lenders on notice—"Feeding time is over!"

5

LOSE THE DEBT NOT YOUR HOUSE

The facts
1. Since 1992-93 the average college graduate's student loan debt has grown from $12,100 to $19,300 in 2003 (inflation-adjusted dollars).
2. Over 25 percent of college graduates in 2003 had student loan debt higher than $25,000, up from 7 percent in 1992-93.
3. In 1983, the median consumer debt for 25-to-34-year-olds was $3,989 (in 2001 dollars). By 2001, the median consumer debt for households under 25 had tripled to $12,000
4. **Twenty nine percent 29%** of low- and middle-income households with credit card debt reported that medical expenses contributed to their current balances.

Mark Brinker. http://www.hoffmanbrinker.com/credit-card-debtstat-istics.html (accessed December 12, 2008).

U.S. consumers racked up an estimated **$51 billion** worth of fast food on their personal credit and debit cards in 2006, compared to $33.2 billion one-year ago. That is a whopping 65% increase in a year. Brad Stroh, http://www.bills.com/consumer-debt-press-release.html (accessed December 12, 2008).

5. Approximately **half** of all credit card holders don't pay the full amount of credit card charges each month. About **11%** say they usually pay only the minimum monthly payment but not much more.

Heather Greer, http://www.PersonalCreditIndex.com. (accessed December 12, 2008).

According to the Federal Reserve Bank, **40%** of American families spend more than they earn.
Kim Khan, http://www.federatedfinancial.com/debtcompare.html (accessed December 12, 2008).

23.8% of American households have no credit cards at all, no bankcards, no retail cards, nothing. **31.2%** of the households paid off their most recent credit card bills in full. Only **one household in 50** carry more than $20,000 in credit card debt. However, that "one in 50 household" figure represents more than 2 million American homes.
Liz Pulliam Weston.http://www.asklizweston.com (accessed January 22, 2008).

Currently 90% of the world's working population is 50-70% in some form of debt as noted in the root cause analysis below:

The findings of an independent commission, chaired by former Downing Street policy chief Lord Griffiths of Fforestfach, include the warning that any major external shock - such as an oil price explosion - would create serious economic and social problems for the 15 million people in the UK who struggle with debt repayments.

According to the Financial Risk Outlook 2005 over a quarter of families have at least one credit card where the outstanding balance is not cleared each month, owing nearly $5,000. On average, this is 14% higher than last year. The student loan company outstanding debt rose sharply. It is now 27% higher than in 2003.

In both a household survey and a survey of the Citizens Advice Bureau (CAB) clients, the top three reasons quoted by those suffering debt problems were:
- Sudden change in personal circumstances—resulting typically from job loss, relationship breakdown, or illness.

- Low income—the consequences of living for a long time on a low level of income.
- Over-commitment—in some cases related to money mismanagement.

The number of consumer debt problems dealt with by Citizens Advice Bureau has risen by nearly three quarters over the last seven years, figures released today by the national problem-solving charity reveal. Consumer debt issues seen in bureaus stood at 706,700 in 2003/4 compared with 405,800 in 1996/7—a rise of 74%. Bureaus dealt with nearly 1.1 million debt-related issues last year, a figure that also includes housing, utilities and benefits-related debts.

However, consumer debt is by far the biggest type of debt problem for which people come for help. A quarter of those in debt are receiving treatment for stress, depression and anxiety from their physician.
Richard Talbot. http://www.creditaction.org.uk.html

National debt and Personal debt have contrasting similarities, because they both represent borrowed amounts that need to be paid, written-off or extended further into the future. American Consumers need to be crusaders in the **War on debt.**

The debt load on the U.S. economy and personal consumer debt has spiraled wildly out of control in recent years. America and Americans need to take extraordinary measures to pay down debt. This load is undermining our personal and national existence.

Losing the debt and not the house is going to be defined in the next recovery. American families are putting more emphasis on security. As we sober up from this recession Americans are more aware that financial security can not be built on debt. The insecurity caused by credit and other debt should be the number one target for termination.

Between Dec. 31, 2000 and Dec. 31 of 2003, *EIR* has projected that the total of U.S. indebtedness rose from 28.80 trillion to 36.85 trillion dollars, an increase of more than 8 trillion dollars, or 28%, in only three years.

Richard Freeman, http://www.larouchepub.com/.html

Debt is **grinding up** the future of American families, manufacturing plants and small businesses.

The national debt is money owed by the federal government to other nations and entities. It is indirectly a debt of the citizens, meaning all Americans. The citizens must ultimately pay it off at some point. National debt consists of government bonds, loans, unfunded liabilities such as pension plan payments and goods and services the government has contracted for but not yet paid. The outstanding debt is only good as long as we keep on consuming foreign goods. America's children and future generation is on the hook for this debt.

The cities in the chart on page 51 are representative of affluent American metropolitan centers that have some of the highest debt free ratios to total city population.

Debt Free Percentage in Largest Cities

CITY	Debt Free Percentage	Population stats	
		CITY POPULATION	APPROXIMATE POPULATION IN DEBT
New York	32%	19,000,000	12,900,000
Los Angeles	23%	3,800,000	2,900,000
Chicago	32%	2,800,000	1,900,000
Houston	37%	2,100,000	1,300,000
Philadelphia	44%	1,400,000	784,000
Phoenix	17%	1,500,000	1,295,000
San Antonio	33%	1,300,000	870,000
San Diego	22%	1,200,000	930,000
Dallas	35%	1,200,000	780,000
Atlanta	27%	486,000	354,000

http://www.idcide.com/lists/us/on-population-debt-free-percentage.html
(accessed September 15, 2009).

Debt can make you feel like you are the only one facing this challenge. The percentages shown above consist of the following:

1. Those that inherited money or made their own wealth
2. Those that have never owned a credit card and pay by cash only
3. Those that manage their money wisely by making common sense purchase and saving decisions

Many consumers still believe that debt-free living is an ideal. There are conflicting opinions on this subject. However, it's just a matter of perspective, which distinguishes the ideal from reality. For those who wish to live debt-free, this is possible. Remember, debt free does not mean living without debt, it infers; managing debt effectively and efficiently. Debt is a tool, not a way of life.

Franklin D. Roosevelt
First Inaugural Address
Saturday March 4, 1933

Seventy-Seven Years ago

Values have shrunken to fantastic levels. Taxes have risen; our ability to pay has fallen; government of all kinds is faced by serious curtailment of income; the means of exchange are frozen in the currents of trade; the withered leaves of industrial enterprise lie on every side; farmers find no markets for their produce; the savings of many years are gone.

Seventy-seven years ago we had troubled assets. What have we learned 77 years later? Lest we forget, our future ties to our past.

"I place economy among the first and most important virtues and debt as the greatest of dangers to be feared." - Thomas Jefferson

"The decline of great powers is caused by simple economic over extension." - *The Rise and fall of the Great Powers*, by Paul Kennedy

*"There is no means of avoiding the final collapse
of a boom brought about by credit (debt) expansion.
The alternative is only whether the crisis should come sooner
as the result of a voluntary abandonment of further credit (debt)
expansion, or later as a final and total catastrophe of the currency
system involved."* - Ludwig von Mises

*"No generation has a right to contract debts
greater than can be paid off during the course of its own existence."*
George Washington to James Madison 1789

*"Growing domestic and international debt
has created the conditions for global economic and financial crises."*
Bank for International Settlements June 2005

For the first 130 years of our nation's history, we possessed little to virtually no debt. Debt began to increase in 1918 because of U.S. involvement in World War I, though the debt decreased in the years that followed.

Following the depression, the debt began an upward slope, due in part to Roosevelt's "New Deal." Beginning in 1942, the debt tripled in just three years because of World War II, and at the end of the war, it dropped.

The national debt peaked at 120% of GDP in 1946 due to the war effort, but Roosevelt, Truman, Ike, Kennedy, LBJ, Nixon and Carter all did their part to bring the national debt back to pre-war levels. By the beginning of 1981, the national debt had fallen to 32.5% of GDP.

To put that in personal terms, a individual with the average U.S. income of $38,000, their share of the national debt is the equivalent of about $12,000 added to their personal debt—sizable but not unimaginable.

The formation of the Global twenty (G20) is a step in the right direction for America to share the world stage with other developed nations. By letting others pay to play, the U.S. will eventually be able to reduce the national debt to pre-and post-WWI &II levels.

6

IT'S ABOUT THE MONEY STUPID

If the government were to send you a letter demanding that you pay your portion of the national debt today, would you have the money to pay them? Worst case, they could tax you or find some other means to get it. The national debt is a real number.

Each citizen under the government's jurisdiction is liable for the national debt. The amount of debt owed per person is computed using the following formula:

$$= \frac{\text{Short Term Debt} + \text{Long Term Debt} - \text{Cash \& Equivalents}}{\text{Population}}$$

The approximate U.S. national debt per person in 2003 was around $17,000 for every man, woman, and child, not counting the state and local debts. You should be able to get the idea regarding your loaded debt burden as a U.S. citizen.

Market statistics on U.S. debt and reserves

- U.S. official gold reserves are worth $261.5 billion (as of March 2008), foreign exchange reserves $63 billion and the Strategic Petroleum Reserve $67 billion (at a market price of $104/barrel with a $15/barrel discount for sour crude).
- The national debt equates to $30,400 per person of the U.S. population, or $60,100 per head of the U.S. working population as of February 2008.
- In 2003, $318 billion was spent on interest payments servicing the debt, out of total tax revenue of $1.95 trillion.

- Total U.S. household debt, including mortgage loan and consumer debt, was $11.4 trillion in 2005. By comparison, total U.S. household assets, including real estate, equipment, and financial instruments such as mutual funds, was $62.5 trillion in 2005.
- Total U.S. consumer credit card revolving credit debt was $937.5 billion in November 2007.
- Total third world debt was estimated to be $1.3 trillion in 1990.
- The U.S. balance of trade deficit in goods and services was $725.8 billion in 2005.

The national debt calculator below shows we owe 50-70% of our earning capacity, which goes to debtors holding the U.S. note.

America and Americans continue to have personal and federal finance challenges that we must overcome at any cost. This market downturn has enlightened us to the fact that we cannot and should not expose ourselves to overreaching debt.

As the economy begins to expand, America and Americans need to discontinue building the future on borrowed money. America needs to do more to balance the budget between consumption and taxation. Everything is OK until the economy shrinks. As the economy contracts, taxpayer dollars is required to keep the economy afloat through recovery. This is a frustrating position to be in, especially when debtor nations lose confidence in the system and start worrying about how America will make good on its expanding debt obligation.

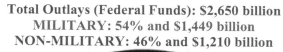

Total Outlays (Federal Funds): $2,650 billion
MILITARY: 54% and $1,449 billion
NON-MILITARY: 46% and $1,210 billion

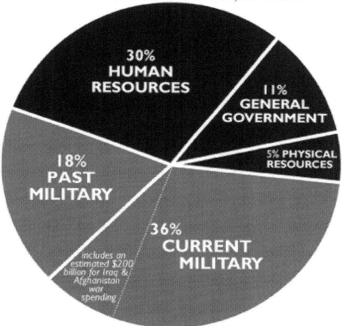

HOW THESE FIGURES WERE DETERMINED

"Current military" includes Dept. of Defense ($653 billion), the military portion from other departments ($150 billion), and an additional $162 billion to supplement the Budget's misleading and vast underestimate of only $38 billion for the "war on terror elements." "Past military" represents veterans' benefits plus 80% of the interest on the debt.

Analysts differ on how much of the debt stems from the military; other groups estimate 50% to 60%. We use 80% because we believe if there had been no military spending most (if not all) of the national debt would have been eliminated.

http://www.warresisters.org/pages/piechart.htm (accessed February 02, 2009).

The pie chart below is the government view of the budget. This is a distortion of how our income tax dollars are spent because it includes Trust Funds (e.g., Social Security), and the expenses of past military spending are not distinguished from nonmilitary spending. For a more accurate representation of how your Federal income tax dollar is really spent, see the large chart (top).

Past Military

$484 billion

• Veterans' Benefits $94 billion

• Interest on national debt (80%) created by military spending, $390 billion.

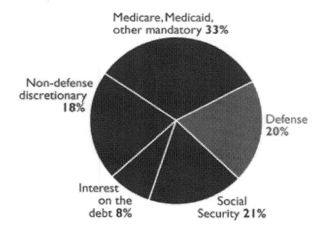

Accumulated Debt/Savings

Borrowed by the General Fund	**10,195,580,425,161**
Income: Income taxes	Outgo: Defense 30%, Interest 19%
Saved by the Social Security Trust	**+2,336,711,305,120**
Income: FICA Payroll taxes.	Outgo: Benefits and disability
Saved by other Gov. Trust Funds	**+4,391,742,569,341**
Income: FICA & gas taxes.	Outgo: Medicare, highways, etc

Debt Held by the Public (net debt)	**-5,803,837,855,819**

http://en.wikipedia.org/wiki/United_States_federal_budget

The U.S. has a larger-than-life war effort going on. Historically our economy has either grown or shrunk when a war effort is in pursuit. The U.S. owes more to other countries financing the debt. Another way to view this is that other countries need us to consume and borrow more.

"This generation feels that somehow they're going to figure out some new advancement that's going to get us out of the financial troubles," says Manning. Professor Manning served as adviser to the forthcoming documentary "In Debt We Trust." The documentary paints a picture of national financial crisis stemming from the personal-debt burden.

Tax revenue is not enough to cover expenditure, so we need to have the following to bridge the gap:
1. Possess abundant natural resources like oil, gas, gold, or some other useful resource.
2. Create a technological or resource advantage, such as we did with flight, automotive, locomotive, internet or other advancements.
3. Borrow more.

America must change her dependence on foreign debt, just as we need to detach ourselves from dependence on foreign oil. Borrowing to support growth is good as long as growth outstrips borrowing. Do we want to sustain this debt dependence over the long-term? There is a lot of talk about the effects on future generations. However, action is essential to provide substantial change. This behavior is unhealthy. It creates a "generational debt" that needs to be reversed. We owe it to our children and future generations. It's going to take a brick-by-brick approach to rebuild financial security and national pride in our economy.

It Makes Sense to Put the Brakes on Excess

American consumers are on the fence when it comes to excess. There are more arguments for it than against it. Successive administrations walk down the same road of increased spending and a ballooning budget deficit. The media promotes more excess to the point where the system overheats and shuts down. Excess is a double-edged sword. Excess has not set a very good example. On the one hand it consumes more than it needs. On the other hand common sense is put on hold to satisfy the need for things. Thank goodness common sense is back in the game.

Now is the time to put the brakes on excess credit, debt and overspending. Good fiscal management is about managing what comes in and goes out. Ideally, your assets should always be in excess of liabilities. What we own needs to be more than what we owe.

It is a well known fact that when there is a storm on the high-seas, merchant vessels unload the cargo to make it through the storm. Consumers must strike a balance to save and build financial security with less debt. Debt is a good head start for buying a house or starting a business. However, at some point a level of independence needs to kick in and reduce the need for debt even when it is convenient.

PART
3

7

MIND OVER MONEY

My wife used to ask me to buy milk at the supermarket. That request only ran for a short period. Every time I would come back with a bag of groceries. That is "irrational spending." Supermarkets love that. My wife was not too pleased. I purchased two pairs of shoes last month. I went back and purchased two more pairs this month. That is "compulsive spending." It's all about mind over money.

Everything seems to be getting smaller these days, including cars, food portions, telephones, and houses. The time is right for credit card and other debt to follow the trend. Everybody likes success, nobody likes a failure. There are so many people failing miserably when it comes to money management. You can win the battle over runaway spending one transaction at a time. Consumers are now forced to rethink how and when they spend their money.

Mind over money is a common sense concept that defines your attitude about spending. **Will it be charge, cash, or no thanks!** Who is in control? Is it your mind or your emotions? If you try to fit a square peg into a round hole, it just will not fit. Giving in to uncontrolled spending reduces the ability to thrive. There needs to be a control mechanism in place. Saying no thanks is a good place to start when faced with a decision to spend further into debt. Should your mind or emotions prevail? The mind is very persuasive and it helps us make the best and worst decisions based on individual circumstances. Common sense is the counter-balance. By engaging your active thinking, you become the best money manager you can be. There is always a solution when common sense is given a chance to think first. An underlying appreciation for engaging common sense prevails when you discover you are in control. It's all about mind over money. Americans are making lifestyle adjustments on many levels. There is still an opportunity to challenge yourself and do more by shaving down to meet your financial range.

Learning to make sound decisions while under pressure to spend requires extra attitude. If you are torn between decisions, rethink.

Financial stability begins in the mind, not the pocket. It's amazing what you can do personally and financially when you rethink before you buy.

Financial freedom results from a change in attitude and thinking. Choose wisely, spend out of need. This will reduce the stress and worry about paying for things today that was purchased several years ago. In a common sense way you can live your best life now.

The goal is to have more financial freedom. That is without a doubt the American way of life. More is good. More is healthy. More education, more jobs, more pay, more healthcare, more peace, more love, more power, more understanding, more respect, more self control and the ability to keep more of your money. Having that insatiable appetite for more has enabled Americans to extend the boundaries of their experiences for the love of God, arts, sciences, humanity, politics and other forms.

What's your pleasure? Common sense money is not about totally denying yourself of the things you need. It's about building stability and financial security. This economic downturn is a reminder of what insecurity feels like. Jane is at a point where her options are shrinking fast. It's important to stay motivated and focused on the issues at hand. Why is that important? We are under observation by our children, friends and family.

A mother went to a supermarket to do her weekly shopping, at the checkout counter; the total cost for her purchases was $252.00. She paid $52.00 in cash and the rest she paid by presenting coupons. Was that a great idea or what? You decide.

A year ago American consumers would have been embarrassed to stand at the store checkout counter scanning coupons. Holding up the line was not something you wanted to do unless you were hoping for a scolding from an impatient customer. Today everybody is doing it!

My wife went to the local supermarket and noticed a lady was trying to decide if she should buy an item. My wife gave her a $4 coupon that was going to expire anyway. The lady was so ecstatic. I never realized that someone could be so happy about a $4 coupon.

What is the most important lesson you will ever learn about money? It's hard to get and harder to keep. Everybody is making demands for your money. You need to manage money efficiently. Money is always available from different sources. Working hard for your money is not the issue. The issue is what you do with the money that you have. Some people treat money like it grows on trees.

If Money Grows On Trees, Where Is The Tree?

Don't waste it, think twice before you spend it, and then use it for things that you need, not just things that you want.
Frank Maguire Times Newspapers Limited. 2008.

Treating oneself is great you deserve it. However, never spend beyond your means to pay. It's the little extravagances that cause the most pain and stress over time. If you are living paycheck to paycheck the road to ruin is paved with extravagances.

8

THINK POSITIVE! BE AN OPTIMIST

If you are a pessimist there is nothing about these current economic conditions to be pessimistic about! We are all at the bottom of the worst economic crisis. It does not get worse than this. Everyone by default is now an optimist. It's time to rethink. No matter how you spin it, being optimistic is the only way up.

The darkest part of the night is always the time before daybreak. The problems are real and the effects on individuals and American families like Jane's keep compounding. The positive changes are just not happening quickly enough to make a visible impact. In these times your attitude counts. Be optimistic. You have done all that is in your power. Let time and a positive attitude do the rest. You only have control over what you can control.

Tough times require the financially fragile to be stronger and committed to a recovery plan like 911 – Common Sense Money. When there seems to be no way out, you must believe. Stand up and fight back when the odds are against you. In this financial crisis, quitting is not an option. The positive side of this crisis is that it focuses our attention on how to be creative and efficient with less.

Companies are already moving into high gear to streamline their processes. They are optimistically thinking and planning ahead for the new wave of economic growth that is on the way. If this were not the case, we should all be worried about the future. Like corporations, consumers need to act on their optimistic convictions.

Your attitude, behaviors and communication should demonstrate an air of optimism. This thinking can help Main Street consumers thrive through the tail end of this economic turbulence and the recovery period. "The fact is Main Street consumers are scared and the only thing they're doing is selling," said Ryan Detrick, senior technical strategist at Schaeffer's Investment Research. "Investors are cleaning out portfolios and getting rid of everything because nothing seems to be working." http://www.nj.com/news/index.ssf/2008/10/stock_market_plummets_more_tha.html (accessed October 09, 2008).

Jane and four million unemployed and financially challenged American men and women struggle to focus on the future as the issues of surviving right now take center stage. How many more families could potentially become unemployed and homeless is a bigger concern. It would appear on one hand that families are losing control due to the economic uncertainty. On the other hand, consumers are controlling the things they can. It's not over until it's over.

This crisis is a big adjustment to every social and economic group. The downsizing by Corporate America is a good example for consumers to follow as they try to adjust to this ever changing environment. Chameleons are reptiles that adapt very well to their environment by changing their color to match their circumstances. Never resist change, just adapt.

Jane continues to adjust her lifestyle and spending priorities to match the current state of her finance. For Jane and millions of American families, this crisis is not an act of choice but of circumstances.

Making the transition from being nearly broke, financially distressed and unemployed to having financial stability can only be successful and sustainable as thinking and outlook change. Smart people act and make sacrifices while others do nothing. Don't be a "do nothing." Making the hard choices essentially says that you are optimistic about your financial security and the economic recovery of this great nation.

Three people stood in an open field on a cloudy day looking. The first person looked down and saw mud. The second person looked up and saw blue sky. The third person just kept looking forward into limited visibility. What are you looking at today? Being an optimist is easy when you are focused on the big picture.

9

RECOVERY ON THE REBOUND

Two thousand and eight was the Year of the Rat. Coincidentally the rat "ate everything." The rat trashed jobs, housing and the economy. Two thousand and nine is the Year of the Ox. Slow and steady is perceived to be good for economic stability. Two thousand and ten is the year of the Tiger, fearless and courageous. Families like Jane are slowly finding the courage to rebuild financial security through common sense cash conservation and savings. This is the premise behind 911 – Common Sense Money. It's about building your financial security one transaction at a time.

This recovery means something special! Unlike other recoveries since the 1930s, it will not be an event that passes by without any personal thought or reflection. You have spent a lot of time and energy making difficult choices and adjustments in your personal finance. The time is coming to reap the rewards of your sacrifice and hard work.

The first part of the recovery is going to be a result of corporate re-engineering, cuts in operational functions and other efficiency drivers. Government stimulus continues to be a big help, even if it is only meant for the short-term. The second part is tied to consumer confidence.

The rate of unemployment is still on the increase, albeit at a moderately slower pace. **Real people are losing jobs every day**. It's not just a number or a statistic—families and communities are affected. There is good news for those that are still working and provides a ray of hope for those out of work. The economic situation is finding its foothold at the bottom. Banks are trying to stabilize their balance sheets, from the impact of the mortgage crisis. There are many programs which allow homeowners to stay in their home despite falling behind on their payments. This is a 360-degree turn from the attitude displayed by banks in the past.

Jane like millions of American families and individuals is looking forward to full economic recovery. The federal government can and will only do so much and go so far. Jane has a personal interest in this recovery. She believes that the success of this recovery is tied to her ability to budget appropriately, manage debt, and secure her families future through this challenging time. The recovery is going to be a natural progression.

911 – Common Sense Money helps you identify existing gaps in your budget and provides a solution to control leakage during the recovery period. These leaks include spending on everything that is not essential to your survival. Reasonable food, shelter and clothing expenditures should be part of your daily guide to survival. Everything else is a questionable expense. Resisting the temptation to hold off on unnecessary spending during the recovery period is difficult but necessary.

When you think you have cut enough personal expenses, think again. There are other ways to be creative and do more. Part of your recovery needs to include shedding as much of the debt baggage as possible. This economic downturn puts a strain on creativity for some and turns on the light for others. A downturn is a terrible thing to waste. Common sense incites that you need to be in a stable financial position to rise with the tide of recovery, not end up staying at the bottom of the river.

Savings continue to rise as consumers spend less and save more. Recovery is on the way up as we see increasing stability and control in personal expenditure and savings. This is good for banks, as they will be more inclined to lend money if consumers have something—that resembles collateral.

Confidence springs from a feeling of security. Financial security is at the heart of recovery. It is estimated that ten percent (10%) of Americans affected by the recession will continue saving and spending in a more controlled and calculated way. Will you be part of that group? Your continued security depends on it. This change in attitude will be seared in the mind of American families, as the lesson of this recession is passed on to future generations.

The federal government is spending its money first then as consumer confidence kicks back, overall spending will increase. It is going to take time for consumers to fully recover. American consumers are far beyond the insinuating market pressures to "grease the wheels of commerce." Families at risk or burned by credit problems, unemployment and foreclosure have learned from this series of events. American families like Jane are very conscious of these incidents occurring again. Therefore, "an ounce of prevention is much better than a pound of cure."

Future consumer spending will be slower than the rate of recovery as budgetary caution becomes part of the decision to spend within a more controlled environment. This attitude will be a new phase in spending than we have seen in past recessions. For Jane and others it will not be "business as usual."

It is so easy to get confused with all the conflicting information about when this recession will end. No one is ready to make the call.

There is no need for you to wait till someone makes the call. Recovery starts in the mind first, not the pocket. Just do your part.

We all get to a point when we need inspiration and motivation to get over the hump. Dig deeper and make sure you get in on the recovery. We are all going to recover in different ways and slightly different times. However, recover we will.

Over thinking on what you need to do can cause stress and anxiety. Don't punish yourself. Keep working at your recovery one transaction at a time. Never stand still just waiting for something to happen—continue to move forward.

Patience is going to be a necessary ingredient through the recovery period. Recovery is not going to happen tomorrow. With patience, you will not be disappointed. Stay focused on the big picture and addresses one transaction at a time. **You only have control over what you can control.**

Financial security comes from hard work and possessing a take-charge attitude. Be practical, realistic and honest with yourself. Create a plan and stick to it. The road ahead is definitely brighter from the bottom looking up. Find inspiration when you do not feel motivated. Americans continue to conserve their way out of this crisis, not spend further into it. Recovery is on the rebound.

The recovery will slowly bring with it boundless opportunities to succeed and thrive. Remember, making money is easy. **Keeping it requires discipline!** Continue the disciplined approach.

Now is the perfect time to reflect on the past and make way for the future. Don't be overtaken by paranoia, or the current roller coaster ride that your personal finances are going through. This phase is ending and another is beginning. This crisis is an opportunity to make meaningful adjustments to rebalance. Make sure your family gets it. Recovery is on the way so be prepared for it. There are four indicators of recovery. They are as follows: stock market gathering momentum, more production, employment and housing growth.

Cleaning up personal debt is preventing and even stalling economic recovery for a very good reason. This is why the recovery will feel like anything but a recovery. Consumer spending on Main Street accounts for seventy percent (70%) of the U.S. economy, and ninety percent (90%) of that is on credit. Americans have tightened their belts on vacation plans, eating out, and forgoing the non-essentials. This recovery is coming from a very deep decline. At times it may appear like nothing is happening. Just believe and be patient, recovery is on the rebound.

10

911 – CASH CONSERVATION

Conserving cash is a sure way to build your nest egg for the future. Common sense tells you that you need the piece of mind and security that nest eggs bring. Conserving cash is not meant to deny self-indulgences. It's about protecting yourself and those that depend on you. Emergencies will come; if you do not have a cushion, then what?

When it comes to cash conservation, the baseline nest egg at ten thousand and above in <u>free cash</u> is what I call the top tier. Ten thousand to two thousand is the middle tier and two thousand to a thousand is the bottom. In the event that you have an emergency, you need to feel secure in one of those tiers.

Think of your cash as an endangered species. Learn to protect it and use it wisely, no matter the cost. Everyone else may be spending theirs. You need to be cautious about spending yours. The reality is that spare change has never been so appealing, as families now struggle to make ends meet.

A working class American family was struggling to meet payments for the electric utility bill. Their son went into his secret box and offered it to mom and dad to pay the bill. The parents reluctantly accepted the box, only after their son became so persistent. The content of the box totaled $400 in change. Their son taught them a valuable lesson about cash conservation. They hoped for more money, but right now, they were willing to settle for saved change.

Have you ever wondered why banks are reporting record earnings in this economic downturn while consumers and small business still struggle to borrow money? Banks are conserving cash until they are comfortable that the recovery is strong enough. Banks lend money in very small amounts and in unique cases only. Case in point, banks are very unwilling to lend to those that are heavily in debt. If you have cash, hold on to it! Don't be so eager to spend it, especially during a period of recovery.

Target Corporations President and Chief Executive, Gregg Steinhafel, told investors during a conference call: "During these tough times, some of our consumers don't want to be tempted as much as they have in the past." Chances are if you need to spend your money so badly, you probably do not need the item at all. Therefore, it is important to take a common sense look at the transaction and rethink before spending.

Ninety percent (90%) of consumer spending comes from impulse buying habits. Corporations are in the business of making money on consumption and compulsive spending patterns fueled by the marketing blitz. It is only natural that shareholders are looking for strong returns on their investment with these corporations.

If the company cannot provide the level of return that the shareholder is looking for, the reality is that stock gets dumped. Companies need the cash infusion. There is therefore a driving incentive to sell to stay in business. Marketing is the key to consumerism, as consumers buy with their eyes and ears. You may accumulate stuff that, in reality, you really don't need. Yes, it is a conspiracy to get you to buy more of what you only need today and stockpile for tomorrow. The question is what are you going to do about it? The cash registers are ringing and you are still paying.

Everyone loves a bargain. To feed the temptation, merchants have made sure that you cannot walk away from a good bargain. Creative advertising and pricing has got everyone hooked. Try saying no for your own financial well-being, rather than indulging in the short-term gratification that you really cannot afford. When the economy is better, spoil yourself. Times are hard, and you owe it to yourself to rethink and adjust to the times. Conservation is a very simple concept; you want to be in the best shape possible when this economic downturn is over.

Cash Is King

Since the beginning of time, cash has played an important role in the commercial exchange of consumer items and services. Cash is king. Cash does two things: one, it gives you the ability to buy and bargain, and two, no long-term debt is attached. Cash creates a disciplined approach to spending money, which makes you live on your terms. One of the main benefits of cash is that it forces you to buy only what you can afford.

There is greater control over spending with cash rather than a credit transaction. With cash, you can see it, smell and touch it. Obviously, there is a greater awareness and sense of responsibility in how quickly it is spent.

Cash gives you access to terms not available to the other person using credit. Cash gives you leverage in markets dominated by recessionary factors.

You can use cash in many instances to leverage your purchases. Some gas stations will reduce their price per gallon if you pay cash not credit. Credit cards cost the vendor. Merchants have to pay the credit card company up to 3% for every transaction you make. Card transaction costs are added back to the sales price of the product. This is why cash is cheaper than credit. Vendors will give you a better deal when cash is used. They save and so do you.

There is an additional cost to the merchant when credit is the method of payment. Credit is beginning to be extremely expensive on the sales and buy side of the transaction. It is just a matter of time before cash will take the reign as king over credit. Consumers who are liquid and have cash are the kings and queens of this recession. Credit card companies are hammering consumers to make revenue. They are squeezing the consumer dry. In the competition for dominance, security and spending power, cash is the way to go. Wisdom is important to strengthen your cash position. Preserve cash at all costs.

It Makes Sense to Have More Disposable Income

Disposable cash income is a necessary "nice to have" after bills are paid. When there is no money left to take care of emergencies or to treat your family, this is an example of zero disposable income, otherwise referred to as living from paycheck to paycheck. Disposable income should increase as your expenses become smaller in contrast to your income. At least five percent (5%) of your wages or benefits should be free and available as disposable income.

When savings increase so will disposable income. Salary increases, bonuses, or other benefits are expected to be flat without any growth in the near future for most Americans. It makes sense to conserve cash. You will not be alone. Everyone is doing it.

Jane now has a few practical common sense ideas to help her turn debt into success and financial freedom. Jane is taking the pressure off her money and her family by living at a level that her income can support. Many Americans are doing this and the results are great. However, sometimes you may have to think outside the box to get to a level of financial control that your income can support.

Your family may be boxed in by the limitation placed on your current finances. Debt and the lack of free cash can place restrictions and stress on families. It's time to break free by thinking outside the box. American families are using this downturn as an opportunity to take the restrictions off their family by making the relevant sacrifices, without the guilt of what others might think. Everybody is doing it!

The solution is conserving as much cash without denying yourself of the basic necessities for daily survival. Remember, your income is fixed and expenses vary from month to month. There is seldom room for change in income, as income becomes stagnant or drops. We have seen a lot of this lately as companies have asked employees to take a pay cut. The irony is that when the economy fully recovers you are starting from a lower base. This is why cash conservation makes sense.

Never cherry pick your expenses when deciding that conserving cash is important. Low hanging expenses have the least impact. Go for those transactions that when a change is made you will see and feel the impact.

A family wanted to go on a vacation to the Caribbean. They had the money but felt guilty about spending that kind of cash in this uncertain economy. My advice was simple. Think outside the box. Downgrade, save some cash, but go on vacation.

Two years ago when cash was plenty, if you came up short, one of your best buddies would gladly give you some. Today cash is tight for everyone. 911 – Common Sense Money provides you with so many tips, so help yourself. It may seem like change but change all adds up. Remember, every penny counts when you need it most.

11

NINETY-ONE 911 TIPS

Is there some place you have forgotten to look for that extra savings? When cash is tight 911 – Common Sense Money wrings out the spare change.

Some advice from Jane: Squeeze the most value from every dollar that you spend. It's American to be thrifty!

Is your cup half-full or half-empty? The following represent valuable 911 – Common Sense tips to save and conserve more money:

1. Ask your doctor for a paper prescription. This gives you the ability to shop around for generic drugs at competitive rates. Electronic prescriptions lock you into a pharmacy and reduce your ability to cut prescription costs. Save $100s every month.

2. When driving at a speed higher than 56 miles per hour with the windows open, you consume more fuel than you would with the air conditioning turned on, due to the increased aerodynamic drag.

3. Reduce medical premiums by selecting specific items to develop your plan. Broad-based coverage makes you pay for anticipated services you have never and may never use. Save $100s on annual premium costs.

4. If the frames for your glasses are in good condition you only need to replace the lens! Save $100s on annual vision costs.

5. Special enrollment medical coverage is better than Cobra after a job loss. This saves on average $3,000 per year. The trick is to apply within 30 days of being unemployed.

6. Defend yourself if you have to go to court for a foreclosure on your home. Lawyers are charging anywhere from $5,000-$15,000 to take the case. Some lawyers are reluctant to take the case because they believe they will not receive compensation. People going through foreclosure are practicing *pro se*—a Latin phrase meaning for oneself. Helpful information for self-defense is available on **Garfield's "Living Lies"** and **"Mortgage Servicing Fraud."**

7. Fuel treatment contains a clean burning additive that adds power, creates fewer emissions and gives you 50 additional miles in extra gas or diesel consumption. Save $100s in annual gas costs.

8. Get 50% off or buy one get 1 free meal at your favorite restaurants anywhere in the U.S. and Canada. Check out Complete Savings.

9. Pack your dishwasher and laundry machine. Half loads use the same amount of energy and water. Save $100s.

10. Community colleges offer the same classes taught at state/private universities for a lower fee per credit hour. The credits are transferable to four-year undergrad programs. Save $1,000s on tuition, travel and boarding costs.

11. Buy your own replacement car parts, and find a mechanic to install. Negotiate labor charge. Save $1,000 in mark-up fees on parts and service costs.

12. If your transmission goes during this recession, do not repair it. Buy a new one. Repair cost: $6,500. New cost: $4,000 – save $2,500.

13. Rubber sole shoes are healthier than synthetic materials. They last 50% longer and reduce the risk of medical expenses caused from foot pain, which later requires therapy. Save $100s in out of pocket medical expenses and additional shoe purchases.

14. Don't put your property tax escrow payments on automatic payment. Insufficient funds will cost you extra fees. Give yourself some flexibility, pay by check. Save $100s in late fees.

15. Pay your mortgage 12 times not thirteen times per year. Save on the five-week months that make up the thirteenth payment. That is over $1,000 you can keep every year.

16. Make sure that your town does not have an alarm ordinance. If you are not registered and your alarm goes off, you will be charged $100 if an officer has to come to your home more than once. Register and save.

17. Reduce your natural gas energy bill by 20%. Rate per therm costs go as low as 0.79 cents. Save $100s.

18. Don't charge your credit card for shipping free products on the internet. Rogues are holding your credit card and rebilling for future shipments that you did not order. Save $1,000s.

19. Parking ticket is a civil case. Municipal courts are offering amnesty programs that drop all additional fees. You just pay the base ticket charge. Save $100s.

20. Friction additive extends your oil change by two thousand miles. Regular oil change runs for three thousand miles. Save $100s.

21. Don't flush your transmission. Empty and refill only. Flushing takes out the sediment buildup that makes the transmission run efficiently. A $160 flush can cost you $3000 in transmission repair.

22. Replace your high interest credit card balance through a Credit Union. Get a rate that is on average 3% lower than the lowest bank rate of 12.5% APR. Save $100s.

23. Take full advantage of interactive Blu-ray features like downloadable live stream video content at a fraction of the cost of Cable TV. Save $100's per month in home entertainment costs.

24. Avoid speeding fines. Travel in packs. You become an easy target when you are isolated and speeding. **Save** $100s.

25. Municipalities are passing ordinances to boot your car after your third parking ticket. It will cost you $50 to get the clamp off and the added inconvenience.

26. Do not cross the white line! The police in a growing number of states will issues tickets if you cross the white line at a red light. Save $100s.

27. Take out insurance on your car loan and credit cards. In the event that you are unemployed, the insurance will pay your monthly payments until you find work. This was a questionable expense until now. Save $1,000s over twelve months.

28. Pay your energy bills online consistently and on-time. Electric companies have programs that will forgo monthly bills at their discretion for good paying customers. Save $100s.

29. De-lamp over lit spaces/rooms in your home. A white wall, for example, has a reflection coefficient of up to 70-80 percent, which can reduce the energy consumed by a lamp. Save $100s on energy and lamp costs.

30. The recommended summer air condition setting is 78 degrees Fahrenheit. Recommended winter setting is 61 degrees. In summer, using an electric fan at the same time allows you to set the air-conditioner to a lower operating level, which can save energy as well.

31. Before you enroll in a college, ask them about any cost cutting programs to help enrolled/enrolling students manage their college expense. Example: using fewer books for classes and offering online courses over the semester. Save $1,000s.

32. Seventy-five billion (75 billion) or 14% of food purchased in the U.S. was thrown away last year. Save $245 per person per family by buying only what you need and protect the environment.

33. When making credit card payments online only hit the send button once! It may appear like the transaction did not take, some systems are just slow or if you are on dial-up then that is slower. If you hit send again you would have paid twice. And you may not get your money back.

34. Late fee waivers are available on your overdue bills. Most companies will give you a complimentary once per year late fee waiver if you ask. Save $100s

35. Use towels to wrap babies bottom, instead of disposable pampers. Save $100s.

36. Only buy term life insurance for the best cost savings up to 75% lower than other policies if you are aged 25-55.

37. Cash for Clunkers. You can deduct the sales tax when you file your taxes for 2009.

38. Grow your own vegetables. The investment in seeds will cost you $60. You can reap annual savings of $1,500 on your vegetable grocery shopping bill.

39. Don't immediately pull the lever at the gas pump. This will cause additional cents on the dollar for your gas charge. Let the pump calibrate and set for two seconds, then pump. Impatience can cost you money.

40. Most cars use premium gas. There was a gas shortage last year in the South. Premium users filled up with regular gas and nothing happened to their cars. You can save on average 20% on each gallon of gas.

41. Soaking rice and other food items in water or marinating meats overnight actually consumes less electricity and cooks faster than cooking non-pre-soaked rice or marinated meats in a 500-watt cooker.

42. Take advantage of FREE water! Buy a water barrel and capture the rainfall from your house. Water plants and wash your car. Work with your environment and save $100s on your annual water and car care bills.

43. If you have store gift cards, use them ASAP. Those stores may not be around when you need them.

44. Get creative. Barter your talents and services for goods and services. Some doctors are giving free medical care for filing, cleaning, bookkeeping, and other services rendered.

45. Frozen meats get freezer burned or ultimately thrown out. Buy fresh, cook and freeze it in parcels. This produces less wastage and reduces food costs.

46. Do not cash out on your investment because of this challenging economy or else you have just **realized your losses**. Stay in until the market regains. Recover $1,000s. The gains will outstrip your losses.

47. Never go food shopping when you are hungry. Hunger drives impulse buying and creates more waste. Save $1,000s per year on food wastage.

48. Hang your clothes on an outside line, if not put them on a drying rack. Save $100s on energy costs generated from clothes dryers.

49. With the equity in your home, refinance over fifteen years, and reduce your monthly payments. Save $100s per month with no closing costs.

50. Buy bulk items from wholesale stores. Split with your family or friend and spread the cost.

51. The average cost to run a car is fifty-four cents per mile. Car pool and save $100s per year.

52. Sharpen your negotiation skills. Anything you buy from a store, ask for additional "discounts offered." You can get a 20% of retail by just asking. Save $1,000s.

53. Monitor the air pressure in tires. The steering system should also be checked regularly in order to make certain it is balanced with the tires. Save $1,000 per year on gas consumption and tire replacements.

54. Switch off and unplug all non-essential electrical appliances like your cable receivers, computers and other gadgets that use energy even when the appliance is off. Save $50 per month in lower electric costs.

55. Convert gas appliances to electric. Electric is 30% cheaper than gas. Get one monthly bill and save $1,000s per year.

56. Buy a pay-as-you-go phone for as little as $60 and only pay for the calls you make. Save $1,000s per year.

57. Get rid of landline phones and go cellular. Save $100s every month.

58. **When was the last time you went to the farmers market?** One way to beat the supermarkets is to eat healthy for less by shopping at your local farmers market is cheaper. They have lower overheads, which translates into cheaper prices. Save $500 every year on vegetable shopping for a family of three.

59. **Do not automatically renew annual travel insurance**. If your annual holiday insurance policy is about to expire and you don't have a holiday booked, DO NOT renew the policy. You wouldn't have car insurance if you did not own a car. Simply restart the cover again the next time you book a trip. Save $100s every renewal.

60. **Renegotiate residential and commercial lease commitments.** Property owners are more open to the idea in an effort to keep occupancy rates high. Demonstrate hardship and get a discount.

61. Instead of thawing frozen food in the microwave oven, consider taking it out the night before and leaving it in the fridge. Speaking of which, fridges should not be jammed packed with things.

62. Leverage home and auto insurance policy to get better rates. Save $100s.

63. Pawning the title to your boat, trailer caravan, is a great way to get quick cash. The key is to get a loan without an early payment penalty so that you can pay off early and get your things back.

64. If you have internet protection services billed to your credit card, renew every year by contacting them within 30 days prior to expiration and ask for a discount. Save 20% on last years cost.

65. If you're a true money-saver, consider an ex-rental car model, which you can pick up for a fraction of the cost of a new one. Save $2,000.

66. **Reason to pack up smoking and drinking:** Never mind the health implication, the guilt or the smell. Your 20-a-day habit is costing you. Save $4,000 every year.

67. If you have a home insurance deductable of $500 increase it to $1,000 and save approximately $150 each renewal term. Save the $150 to cover the additional $500 deductable increase—the rest is pure savings.

68. **Cut cable costs**. Telephone-based services for system checks and updates are cheaper than going through the receiver. Save $50 per year.

69. Cut cable TV packages from $130 a month to $40 per month. Switch around a couple of programs. Delete the ones you do not watch often. Negotiate and save $100s every month.

70. A small car idling for 1 minute consumes more fuel than restarting the car. So if the car has to stop for a long while, turn off the engine. During three (3)

minutes idle time the engine uses enough fuel to power the car for two thirds of a mile.

71. **Avoid the payment protection racket.** Banks and other lenders are selling expensive insurance policies to cover loan repayments to people who don't need it. Do not be a victim of the hard sell. Save $200 every year.

72. **Life insurance payouts should fall in a range that is five to ten times your annual salary.** If you are paying premiums for more than ten times cut back and save.

73. **Avoid extended warranties.** Electrical goods are more reliable than ever. If your new radio won't last three years perhaps it's not worth buying it in the first place. Think about it: How many times has your fridge broken down in the last five years? Moreover, do you really need the hassle of claiming for repairs to a $15 toaster? Save $100s.

74. **Childcare:** If childcare is getting to be a concern financially, hook up with your other friends and find someone that you know who is reliable, trusting, safe and out of work. Ask that person to take care of your child at a fraction of the cost. Just make sure they have certain documentation as required by your state.

75. Ground beef is very versatile and can be used in many dishes like chili, burgers, lasagna, stews, and soups. All these items can be frozen for future use. Save $100s on food shopping costs.

76. Buy kids clothes a size bigger so they grow into it and prevent buying twice. Save $100s every year.

77. Buy food that you can afford by trading down from food that is more expensive to cheaper brands. Save $1,000s.

78. Dry-clean shirts for less than $1. Pay $2 dollars per piece for pants. Dresses cleaned for $5. Check your local listing. Save $100s.

79. The simplest and most effective way to maintain your car is to change the engine oil regularly. The smaller the engine, the smaller the volume of engine oil, which means the oil will need changing more frequently.

80. Save 25% on Unlimited and Simply Everything mobile discount plans when your phone contract is up for renewal.

81. Hard times produce an increase in the crime rate. PROTECT your valuables. Get a safe deposit box. Savings: priceless.

82. Ask your bank for a rate reduction on safe deposit boxes. Banks are cutting box rates by 50%.

83. Kids grow so fast that it is cost efficient to rotate clothes between like siblings and other close family members and friends. Save $100s every year.

84. Don't call family members and friends on separate calls! Rotate conference calls and help your friends and family. Save $100s.

85. LED light bulbs cost more, but they have a longer life than normal incandescent bulbs and they eat far less electricity. Significantly trims your electric bill.

86. **Banks now have programs where for every transaction you make on the bankcard, a dollar is transferred and matched to your savings account. Ask your bank for details. The trick is to get the dollar and keep the transactions low.**

87. Enjoy group discounts on kids' summer camps by joining up with your neighbors and friends. Save $100s.

88. Wait until about two days after a holiday, and then go out shopping for items you need that are themed for that day. Get a Mother's Day card for next year the day after Mother's Day.

89. Request a waiver on cancellation fees tied to any of your expense-related transactions. If you want out there is no penalty for cancellation.

90. Thanksgiving and Christmas sales are going to start earlier in the year. Wait until the days before, and save up to 50%. Don't get sucked in.

91. Home monitoring security contracts are negotiable, when your contract is up; there are brand name companies that will provide you the hardware and installation at no cost. Save

$500 on equipment purchases, and an additional 20% on systems monitoring fees

There Are Ninety-One Different Ways For You To Save And Reduce Your Expenses. Challenge Yourself To Find More!

A friend told me that he will take all the help he can get! Here are a couple more tips.

Tire purchases used to be expensive, but not anymore. You can pick up a slightly less than perfect set of tires at the used tire store for $160. This is $280 less than a brand new set. You can practically get the same mileage as new tires. Used tires come off leased cars or from the factory.

Go on the internet if you have a check engine light or code showing on your car. You can save $100s in diagnostic costs.

Pay all your bills online. Save $100s on increasing stamp and envelope costs.

Entertainment ticket resellers earn their living by getting hold of tickets that are otherwise unavailable. Simply sign up to for the free ticket alert newsletters from the main agents to ensure that you're first in line. Save $100s.

Bundle Internet, cell and landline services. Save $100s.

Sell overstock items in your basement and attic on consignment. Recover $100s.

Create your own vacation with family or friends and split the travel and board costs.

Do you really need two cars, a bike, and a truck? Think about all the other costs to support that fleet; there is an opportunity to save $1,000s every year.

Save 20% on winter heating bills by purchasing an "heat surge." This is a revolutionary home heater created by the Amish.

2010 there will be a zero federal estate tax levy.

If you have coupons that are expiring, give them to someone that will benefit from it.

The Christmas lottery: Instead of trying to buy a present for every relative in your family, consider getting together beforehand and picking one name from the hat. You then buy one thoughtful gift for that one person rather than attempting to please everyone at considerable cost. Everyone gets a present; everyone saves money.

Trying to keep up appearances is little more than a costly illness. Remember, you cannot judge someone by what they have because you don't know how they got it. Chances are they're in more debt than you are. Save $1,000s.

If your neighbor likes landscaping or painting, use them as a resource. Buy the materials yourself and save $1,000s on maintenance costs.

Save 65% on oil change and tire rotation in your local area. Regular cost $35.00. The average discounted cost is $23.00 including tax.

Applying these tips will help to put the brake on excessive spending and increase your disposable income. Wring out the savings and thrive.

Fees for bounced checks and withdrawing cash from an out-of-network ATM rose again this year, according to Bankrate.com. The cost of using another bank's ATM is now $3.43. That is definitely a deterrent and another reason to keep your eye on your money

Eliminating sacred cows can also help lower your monthly expenses. Sacred cows are the things held on to no matter what the economy or personal hardships being felt. They are the things most loved and deemed untouchable. Here are a couple of things:

1. Cable TV (if you can't pay your other bills, then this is a luxury you need to scale down on)
2. The daily newspaper
3. Club membership dues
4. Buying the overpriced lunch every day
5. Magazine subscriptions
6. Lawn treatment
7. Car wash
8. First showings of the latest movies
9. Acrylic nails
10. Event tickets

We all have specific indulgences. Are they sacred to you? Is it practical and necessary right now? Take care of your necessities: food, clothes, and shelter. Adjust your priorities so that food, clothing, and shelter are not last on your list of needs. Cutting costs can be hard but it can also be a fun life experience. Especially when the family is involved and a big picture view is in place. One friend of ours finally gave up his daily newspaper habit, saving $30 each month only to discover that someone brought it to the office every day to share and it was free! The moral in the story is that **every bit counts**.

Every bit counts as the federal government steps in to help consumers by preventing the credit card companies from wringing the spare change out of you. The office of thrift management is heading up this legislation. The new rules entail the following:

1. Stop banks or credit card companies from increasing the interest rates on consumer credit over and above their ability to pay.

2. Stop financial institutions from taking away existing balances or reducing them and in the process affecting consumers' credit scores.

3. Prevent consumers from going into a higher risk bracket because of this scam.

4. Place fair time constraints on payments. A payment could not be deemed late unless the borrower is given a reasonable period, such as 21 days, to pay.

5. No more placing too-high fees for exceeding the credit limit solely because of a hold placed on the account.

6. Stop unfairly computing balances known as a computing tactic, or **double-cycle billing**.

7. Prevent unfair adding of security deposits and fees for issuing credit.

8. Prevent deceptive offers for credit.

9. In addition, consumers will need to have forty-five days' notice before any changes to the terms of an account can be made, including slapping on a higher penalty rate for missed or late payments. Under current rules, companies in most cases give 15 days' notice before making certain changes to the terms of an account.

Finally, the federal government through this piece of legislation will **save you $1,000s** per year in late fees higher interest and interest penalties.

This new law will come into effect in 2010. Until then, credit card companies will continue to take advantage of consumer's hard luck.

Consolidate Debt

Consolidating all your cards into one debit and a credit card is an excellent way to reduce the excess fees and interest on the other cards. You can use them both interchangeably and you will discover that you have more than enough to meet your monthly needs. Your overall debt will go down dramatically as your monthly fees and charges go away. You will save $100s per month in saved fees and interest.

Consolidating credit card debt is the cleanest way to squeeze more savings out of your money. Jane consolidated and only carries one debit and a credit card. Jane has never looked back. There are no more hassles and headaches. Jane now keeps more of her money where it belongs, in her bank.

You may not believe this but banks are still reducing the rates on credit cards especially if you can produce a good case for the reduction. One good pitch is to present a plan to consistently pay an amount for the next six months. Cut a deal to get your rate adjusted. Speak to a supervisor and make a request for a "consolidated" interest rate. The average interest rate on all your cards will be more than a single rate after the consolidation. That is how you thrive and save when you are in debt. Get a financial institution to assume your debt. A lot of people will say: been there, done that! What they have not done is to lock the consolidation to that one card. They get more cards and take on more debt.

On a $20,000 balance, even a 3% rate reduction saves you <u>$600 per year</u>. Consolidation reduces the spread on your money. Build history, then your bank will work with your consolidation efforts. They are always looking for ways to reward loyalty.

Consolidating your debt into one monthly payment is a great way to save big on expenses. There are two main advantages. First, you only pay one monthly bill. The second benefit is that you get a better rate that reduces your interest payments by at least three percent (3%). Three percent (3%) reduction on a monthly interest-only mortgage payment of one thousand dollars ($1,000) equals a $30 per month reduction in interest. It may not sound like a lot, but over the term of the loan, this number becomes a no-brainer in this economy.

Taking the debt consolidation option gives you a fresh start. It works by refinancing your home, using the equity. Refinance with your current lender—the fees are much lower. The bank will also offer you discounts like free safe deposit boxes, check stock replacements and other goodies for your loyalty.

Debt consolidation can work for you and save you thousands of dollars over the long term.

Lenders know that consolidation is a great benefit. They just fail to promote this as an option. This reduces the amount of income over the long term that they can generate from you. When consolidation takes place, banks lose revenue. If it's right for you, pursue it. Budget control is the key to managing a successful consolidation arrangement. Eighty-five percent of debts consolidated fall apart after the first year.

Debt consolidation is a smart choice—especially with the lowest rates in years as banks continue to compete to keep your business. I have not seen a bank that has told any customer to take their business somewhere else! This is a smart method to wring more value out of banks and save.

You spent years building a relationship with your bank. Now is the time to leverage it. Your bank is the best place to get help in times of economic and personal financial need. Use your bank as your resource, not as a last resort. Your bank will work with you before you get into a crisis with a debt problem. You can get all the help that you need on the best terms available. If you need help, ask for it. Speak to the branch manager, not customer service.

You can save a lot of money and time by working with your bank rather than going to a financial institution where there is no history. Your history with the bank allows you to at least discuss the matter. Getting a new bank to attend to and understand your financial needs in this economic climate is very difficult. Work with what you have.

You can't get out of a ditch by digging into it! The bank is your helping hand. Take it.

Points for Purchases

When requesting a credit card, always get one that gives you points for everything that you purchase. This is a great way to get merchandise that you would not normally buy. These goods and services are discounted at an affordable price as merchants continue to compete for your business.

Points for purchase credit cards are an incentive to buy and collect redeemable points. A typical twenty thousand redeemable points can buy many things at no extra cost. Five thousand points gives you a fifty-dollar ($50) voucher for restaurants. Five thousand points gives you a $100 voucher towards car rental and thirty thousand can fly you anywhere in the USA. However, be careful as all points have an expiration date based on the time they are awarded.

Redeem the points before they expire. Check with your card company to find out what the expiration policy is for the points awarded. Use them before you lose them. Remember, every penny counts.

Ten Minutes to Cool Off

Stop before you shop. You can save by waiting ten (10) minutes after the urge to spend. This brief period allows you to think rationally about the transaction. Never shop in the heat of the moment. Quite often, you will find that you really don't need it. Cooling off works!

> Managing debt effectively is the same as living debt free. Investing and savings wisely can accumulate to a small fortune over time.

How do banks do it? Banks as a rule of thumb will lend you 20% of their own reserve; the other 80% comes from other banks or lenders. When you understand how banks make money, you can apply the same principle and make money for yourself. You make money when you become a lender to the bank through money market funds, savings and CDs. All these funds are low risk and medium return funds.

Bank A makes money by borrowing from Bank B at a 1% interest rate. Bank A provides 20% of the loan amount as collateral. Say the loan is $100,000.00. Then Bank A lends out all the $100,000.00 with interest at 2%.

The return will be $2,000.00. Out of $2,000.00, Bank A will pay back $100,000.00 + $1,000.00 (interest) to Bank B, keeping the other $1,000.00 for itself as the return on investment. Since Bank A only put up $20,000.00 (collateral to secure the loan) and gets $1,000.00 return, it actually makes a 5% return on investment ($1,000.00 on top off $20,000.00).

It is interesting to note that Beaumont Pearce the Chairman of Lloyds Bank of England said in Melbourne on 13/11/1934 and shown in the National Bank (NAB) Monthly Summary for December 1934, "that **no capital is necessary to start a bank**." There are many other Parliament Reports showing banks create money out of thin air and the river of interest flowing back to them (sweat interest) is overwhelming. The interest and fees they charge appears to be crippling humanity now.

http://www.discusseconomics.com/banking/where-do-banks-get-their-money/

Banks actually create money when they lend it. Here is how it works. Most bank loans go back to the bank and deposit in their checking accounts.

Loans eventually become a new deposit just like a paycheck does. The bank once again holds a small percentage of that new amount in reserve and again lends the remainder to someone else, repeating the money-creation process many times. Squeeze the banks as much as you can by pushing for higher returns on your available cash.

Refinancing

The most popular method to save money through refinancing is by rate reduction with or without term extension. The rate reduction option reduces the monthly interest, fees and out of pocket expense. The term option pays off the old loan and a new agreement becomes effective for a shorter time. The borrower receives a new contract with an easier term for payoff. Money should not be taken from the refinance for shopping.

The benefit is that the term of the mortgage is lower, so if you paid three years of a 30-year mortgage and refinance at 15 years you have cut off twelve years and can practically pay the same monthly amount and roll the closing cost in the loan amount. The savings is endless. Term adjustment is a great cost-saver, especially if you are close to retirement.

The following is a demonstration:

Rate reduction: - $100,000 mortgage x 2 % interest rate reduction = $2000 annual savings.

Term reduction: – 30-year fixed rate with 25 years remaining. You take no money from the refinance exercise. Your refinance creates a new term from 25 to 15 years. You have essentially created a shorter debt term, thus leaving yourself with 10 years of free cash.

Dos and don'ts you need to know when applying for a refinance:

1. Are there any outstanding judgments against you?
2. Have you declared bankruptcy in the past 7 years?
3. Have you had property foreclosed upon or given title or deed in lieu of foreclosure in the last 7 years?
4. Are you a party to a lawsuit?
5. Have you directly or indirectly been obligated on any loan, which resulted in foreclosure, transfer of title in lieu of foreclosure or judgment?
6. Are you obligated to pay any alimony, child support or separate maintenance?
7. Is your down payment also a loan?
8. Are you an endorser or co-maker of a note?
9. Have you owned property in the past three years?

There is only one problem with refinancing and that is banks will only do this once. Therefore, it is important to make the most of the opportunity and gain the maximum possible benefit from the deal.

12

EYE ON YOUR MONEY

Living on a budget is the only safe and practical way to keep an eye on the money. Without budgets, countries, governments and corporations would be in chaos. Budgets are necessary if you are serious about financial security for you and your family. Here is how budgets work: A budget measures how close you are to your goal. Budgets give you the "heads-up" to make timely adjustments so you stay on target.

Writing checks with the hope that when they clear the system in three (3) days, the money will be there to cover it is not a common sense way to manage your budget. Consumers get burned by late fees and penalties for checks drawn against insufficient funds. It is smarter to let your creditor know that you have difficulty in meeting the payment than to send a check they cannot cash. You need to know that you have money in the bank or not. It is not only embarrassing, but it also affects your credit.

Budgets help you to stay in the black and out of the red. Budgets are not based on wishful thinking; they are based on facts. A graphical illustration helps one to visualize and control cash in and cash out. All successful corporations and families live on budgets. Never underestimate the power of the budget. If you require a loan, banks want to know if your budget is strong enough to absorb the additional expense. If you want to get ahead financially, you need to live by a budget.

Everyone likes a car that runs well on the road as it takes you from point A to point B. Your budget should be that—dependable and reliable when you need it most.

The median salary in the U.S. is about $40,000. You take home $2,500 a month and your monthly expense as an example is as follows:
- ✓ $300 paid installment on revolving loan and other credit
- ✓ $500 car note
- ✓ $1,000 house note or rent
- ✓ $400 property taxes
- ✓ $300 utility and telephone
- ✓ $400 other miscellaneous

As part of your budget plan the following are smart steps to take should you find yourself in a cash short position:

Don'ts:
1. Ignore creditors
2. Concentrate payment to one vendor
3. Panic in a crisis
4. Put off what you can do today for tomorrow

Dos:
1. Make a good faith effort to pay something to everyone
2. Keep creditors happy
3. Should your circumstances deteriorate connect with your creditor
4. Answer creditors' calls
5. Supplement your income with a part-time job for additional cash if at all possible
6. Indulge in a low cost hobby
7. Put off immediate excessive gratifications

Put 10% of your take-home pay towards paying off two of the highest bills you have, and split another 20% across the other outstanding balances. Do this for a year and slash your interest payments by 100%. How does that work? Your average interest rate is 25%; you should be paying 30%. Thirty percent on bill payments is the recommended amount to reduce debt in the short term.

(1) Priority number one is to pay above the minimum required balance shown on your statement for high balances. Additional payments made cover compound interest and some of the principal you owe.

(2) Priority number two is to pay minimum balance requested on the remaining creditors. This strengthens your overall credit rating and shifts the focus to paying down high balances first, then attacking the remaining debt balance one transaction at a time.

One year after consistently paying 30% of your net income to cover debt, you should be able to request a rate reduction. You have now positioned yourself for an annual percentage rate (APR) lower than the current 25%. The concept is very simple: **short term pain, long term gain**. You put out some extra for the short term, and gain in the long term. In this down economy, banks are still reducing rates and fees by 10% to selected customers that have revolving loan payments. You can qualify for lower rates. It just takes a little extra effort.

On a twenty-four percent (24%) APR, every dollar transaction you make, you owe twenty-four cents in interest. Consumers who have better payment histories get the best rates which can be as low as 14% APR. 14% is your target! Make it your goal.

Cut Your Interest Rate and Save 45% on Monthly Interest Payments

How does it work?

Assumptions:

Scenario 1- Credit cards - $20,000@24% APR for 1 year
Scenario 2- Credit cards - $20,000@14% APR for 1 year

Pmt	Cur APR	Adj. APR	Total Cost	Savings
$20,000	24%	**$4,800**	**$24,800**	
$20,000	14%	**$2,800**	**$22,800**	**$2,000**

$2,000 reported savings represents an equivalent 45% (2,000/4,800 = 45%) reduction in annual interest charges and fees. The return on your sacrifice to reduce revolving credit balances calculates as follows:

A
Monthly take home pay = $2,000
Debt owed = $7,200
Thirty percent of pay towards debts = $600 per month
Personal Sacrifice 12x$600 = $7,200 per year
Pay debt in full within 1 year and have $600 spare per month.
B
Reduced interest rate from 24% to 14% equates to $2,000 annual savings
Debt = $7,200/$2,000 = Three and a half years
Pay debt in full in three and a half years and have $2,000 spare per year

Within three and a half years, you will start seeing savings of $2,000 per year as illustrated in example B. You will benefit from $600 extra per month after year one, using example A.

Who needs to wait for a stimulus when you can get that type of money through your own effort? This is a confidence booster. The good thing about this method is that you can repeat this over your total debt load until you are back in control.

Create a visual reminder of your debt. As your debt grows smaller, your wealth will increase. Debt and wealth are opposites. Make a giant progress thermometer that starts with zero progress on your overall debt. Track the percentage change each time. Get the family involved by allowing a member to record the progress being made on the thermometer.

Keep this debt reduction reminder in a place where you will all see it often. Have a family discussion about how each member can contribute to the success of the exercise.

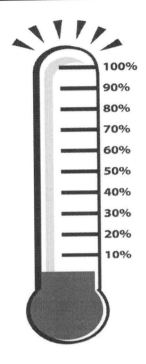

The chart illustrated below is based on a three-month family income and expense budget for Jane. This shows the power of the budget process at work and the benefits derived from its consistent use. February and March show that this family made their best effort to reduce some of their spending patterns. In March this family is about to "break even."

Monthly Actual Expense	Jan	Feb	Mar
Grocery	$400	$400	$200
Gasoline	$300	$300	$200
Utilities	$220	$220	$150
Cell Phone	$100	$100	$100
Gym fees	$80	$80	$0
Entertainment	$150	$50	$55
Clothing	$220	$220	$50
Home Improvement	$200	$50	$0
Loan and other credit	$300	$200	$200
Car note	$300	$300	$300
House note or rent	$1,000	$1,000	$1,000
Total Expense	$3,270	$2,920	$2,255
INCOME	($2,000)	($2,000)	($2,200)
NET LOSS	**$1,270**	**$920**	**$55**

To really make this budget look good, the cost and percentage breakdown of expenses against the two thousand dollar income should look something like this:

Housing Expense $760 or 38% of income
Bills $600 or 30% of income
Food and other $300 or 15% of income
Miscellaneous $200 or 10% of income
Savings $140 or 7% of income

The budget illustration above tells Jane that it's time to move to a new home or renegotiate the house payments to an amount that fits in her budget. The housing cost is eating at her overall income. This is also her biggest expense.

Consumers in general are reactive by way of stimulation of the senses. The need to see things demonstrated in pictorial format tends to get our attention very quickly and motivates us to action. By seeing, one believes. Budgets help consumers to understand the "value of a dollar."

JANE SAVES OVER $1,000 AFTER THREE MONTHS ON THE BUDGET

Monthly Actual Expense	Jan	Feb	Mar
Groceries	$400	$400	$200
Gasoline	$300	$300	$200
Utilities	$220	$220	$150
Cell Phone	$100	$100	$100
Gym Membership	$80	$80	$0
Entertainment	$150	$150	$0
Clothing	$220	$220	$0
Home Improvement	$200	$200	$0
Revolving credit	$300	$300	$400
Car note	$300	$300	$300
House note or rent	$1,000	$1,000	$800
EXPENSE	$3,270	$3,270	$2,150
INCOME	($2,000)	($2,000)	($2,200)
NET LOSS	$1,270	$1,270	($50)

AC Nielsen the media giant, indicates that 22% or approximately one out of five Americans do not have a nest egg. Budget controls can help to build that nest egg one transaction at a time.

Futile savers
Countries with the most consumers who have no spare cash

Country	% of consumers with no spare cash
United States	22%
Portugal	22%
Canada	19%
United Kingdom	17%
France	16%
Netherlands	15%
Turkey	14%
Germany	13%
Chile	12%
South Korea	12%

Source: ACNielsen

Budgets create stability and awareness. Budgets are a visual to help arrange your financial priorities by comparing your income to expenses. The key to a balanced budget is to be able to at least break-even. What you put out should be no more than what you take in. Illustrated in the chart below are the basics of a budget control outline for your convenience.

If for some reason, you go over your budget limit by 10%, it is not a big deal. <u>You have not failed</u>. The great thing about budgets is

that they take into consideration all spending patterns over a period. There will always be patterns of higher and lower expenses. Your expenses should be trending lower as you establish strong spending controls.

There is no need to sweat the small stuff. Check your budget monthly. A thorough review of your budget target is required every six months. If you are running off course in the first six months, you have the last six months to get back on track. Any difficulties in income and expenditures in any given month will even out over the twelve-month cycle—just keep spending as tight to budget as possible. Having a big picture focus is more important than worrying about fluctuations in your spending pattern. There will always be highs and lows.

Budgets are very useful and with much practice will become part of your routine financial checkup. Budget checkups are necessary and fun. Try to see the value of a budget as you continue your conquest to shave and save.

Get the whole family involved in the budget process. Make it a family project so that you can all participate in the quest to make a difference in your family finances.

Celebrate the success together. There is something special about getting family members involved. Make them part of the solution. There is nothing demeaning when it comes to shared responsibility especially when the whole family is affected.

Typical Average Family in Georgia

Atlanta-Sandy Springs-Marietta, GA HUD Metro FMR Area

Two Parents, One Child

Item	Cost
Monthly Housing	$824
Monthly Food	$514
Monthly Child Care	$572
Monthly Transportation	$401
Monthly Health Care	$319
Monthly Other Necessities	$322
Monthly Taxes	$394
Monthly Total	$3344
Annual Total	$40133

Economic Policy Institute, http://www.epi.org/content/budget_calculator

Below is an example of the budget process. The three-month budget illustrates how to control, manage and effectively adjust your expenses, to meet your financial goal.

This is a great exercise for the entire family. The younger members of your family will thank you one day for the experience.

You will notice that March runs into the red, because of the winter expenses. Without this level of detail, it is hard to figure out the gaps in your finances until it is too late. As you can see budgets are all about early detection and prevention.

Budget Worksheet	JAN	FEB	MAR	TOTAL
Income Categories				
Take Home Pay	3,000.00	3,000.00	3,000.00	9,000.00
Bonuses				0.00
Gifts Received				0.00
Tax Refunds				0.00
Interest Income				0.00
Dividends				0.00
Refunds/Reimbursements				0.00
Savings Withdrawal				0.00
Other Income #1				0.00
Other Income #2				0.00
Other Income #3				0.00
TOTAL INCOME	3,000.00	3,000.00	3,000.00	9,000.00
Tax Deductible Expenses				
Business Expenses				
Unreimbursed				0.00
Office At Home				0.00
Other Business Expenses				0.00
Charitable Contributions				
Religious	300.00	300.00	300.00	900.00
Other Non-Profit			100.00	100.00
Deductible Tax				
Personal Property Tax				0.00
Real Estate Tax	350.00	350.00	350.00	1,050.00
Other Deducible Tax				0.00
Health				
Medical Insurance	400.00	400.00	400.00	1,200.00
Medicine/Drug				0.00
Doctor/Dentist/Optometrist	200.00		350.00	550.00
Hospital				0.00
Other Health	200.00		500.00	700.00
Alimony				0.00
Losses-Un-reimbursable				0.00
Mortgage Interest	1,000.00	1,000.00	1,000.00	3,000.00
Other Deductible				0.00
Total Deductible Expenses	2,450.00	2,050.00	3,000.00	7,500.00

Non Tax -Deductible Expenses

Auto/Transportation				
Fuel	150.00	200.00	120.00	470.00
Service	50.00			50.00
Transportation				0.00
Other		100.00		100.00
Utilities				
Electricity	125.00	145.00	102.00	372.00
Gas	200.00	250.00	245.00	695.00
Internet				0.00
Oil/Fuel				0.00
Telephone	150.00	150.00	150.00	450.00
Trash Pickup				0.00
Water/Sewer				0.00
Other Utility				0.00
Vacation/Travel				0.00
Total Non-Deductible Expenses	675.00	845.00	617.00	2,137.00
TOTAL EXPENSES	3,125.00	2,895.00	3,617.00	9,637.00
Income - Expenses	-125.00	105.00	-617.00	
Beginning Balance	500.00	375.00	480.00	
Predicted Ending Balance	375.00	480.00	-137.00	
Actual Ending Balance			-137.00	

13

SQUEEZE THE MONEY OUT OF FORECLOSURE COSTS

More recently, the House and Senate have been working on a more aggressive bailout, which calls for the Federal Housing Administration to insure up to $300 billion in distressed mortgages, which would help about 500,000 homeowners avoid foreclosure.

The proposed legislation also offers a zero-interest 15-year loan for first-time homebuyers. Many have taken advantage of the $8,000 housing stimulus handout, care of Uncle Sam.

There is an extended $15 billion in additional assistance to help state and local governments buy and repair abandoned homes. The most sweeping new program was announced on November 11, 2008.

Freddie Mac and Fannie Mae, the government agencies that guarantee 31 million U.S. mortgages, will begin paying the mortgage service companies that maintain the loans $800 for every loan they modify. This proposal gives some hope to those that are about to go into foreclosure.

Borrowers will get help in several ways: Interest rates will be lower so that borrowers will not pay more than 38% of their gross income on housing expenses. This control is a great step forward to help homebuyers. The 38% represents mortgage payments only. Another option is for loans to be extended from 30 years to 40 years, and for some of the principal amount to be deferred interest-free. Not entirely a great idea. Your advantage is to pay on a shorter term, not to extend further out. Any new changes should be a step up from where you are right now. Paying the debt over a shorter term guarantees long-term savings and will end the debt sooner. Term extension options should be off-limits, as this puts the homeowner back instead of forward to a new start. There is so much evidence which indicates that retired Americans are still paying for housing debt well into retirement. The Federal Housing Administration (FHA) proposal is still the best relief yet for the homeowner.

Nearly 10 million homeowners are having trouble making their mortgage payments, according to Moody's Economy.com. The proposed changes in bankruptcy rules could help as many as 800,000 troubled borrowers keep their homes, estimated by Mark Zandi, chief economist at Moody's Economy.com.
http://www.calculatedriskblog.com/2008/02/economycoms-zandi-on-homeowners-with.html (accessed February 22, 2008).

The push to modify bankruptcy laws comes as the housing market continues to weaken. The bill would allow bankruptcy judges to lower the principal and interest rates on mortgages, and to extend the terms of the loans. It would represent a major shift of power from lenders to borrowers who do not receive any allowance under current bankruptcy law to renegotiate their primary mortgages.

It makes good business sense for banks to be more accommodating in times of financial crisis. Moreover, there is pressure being placed on banks to "open the safe" and help struggling customers prevent foreclosure, which becomes burdensome and expensive for all parties. For the bank and the customer, "prevention is more cost effective than foreclosure."

Foreclosure is an expensive endeavor. Banks have to absorb an increase in management, legal, and other fees to keep and dispose of a foreclosed home. Foreclosures continue despite government intervention. Homeowners are still waiting for banks to fully implement the mortgage relief program.

It makes sense to keep bugging the bank. New programs to help homeowners hold on to their home and reduce the increasing risk of foreclosure are being put in place.

Another mortgage in distress equates to lost revenue for the bank. Homeowners have put their money, time, and energy into their piece of the American dream. It's your dream—don't give up on it. The banks and loan companies will always keep sending those delinquent letters. However, they will never foreclose as long as you pay something. If you are behind on payments, you are not delinquent.

Many would say the common sense thing to do is to cut your losses. Where is the common sense in cutting your losses? You still need to live somewhere and pay rent. If you can pay the rent, why not pay some of the mortgage? At the end of the day it's yours. That makes sense!

Foreclosure should only be pursued when no other alternative is available. There are many examples of homeowners who have not attempted to address their payment challenges earlier on with the lending company. In the past, it has been the norm to give the key back because that is the easy way out. Today there is a more formal process to prevent homeowners from abandoning their investment. **The information provided on this new homeowner, loan modification bailout provides hope to homeowners teetering on the brink**. Don't give up; this is the light at the end of the tunnel!

Help! Main Street consumers need to say so more often. Lending institutions will work with you. It is in the bank's best interest to keep you in your home, even if it means going through a modification program. Keeping your home and your investment in it is the most effective long-term solution where everyone benefits. To make sure homeowners do not bite off more than they can chew, there will be government regulation to some degree for more transparency in the credit and lending markets.

Banks, financial institutions and consumers can save on foreclosure costs if they continue to work together. By far, prevention is cheaper than foreclosure. Without trust, confidence is weak. It takes years to build trust and one day to tear it down.

"Foreclosures hurt families, communities and the overall housing market," said James Lockhart, the housing finance agency's director. "We need to stop this downward spiral."
http://www.marketwatch.com/news/story/story.html (accessed December 12, 2008).

Fannie Mae and Freddie Mac own or guarantee nearly 31 million U.S. mortgages or nearly six of every 10 outstanding mortgages. Still, government officials did not have an estimate of how many people would qualify for the new program.

Officials hope that the new approach will go into effect soon. This will be a model for future loan-servicing companies which collect debts owed to mortgage companies and distribute to investors.

Loan-servicing companies are facing criticism for being slow to respond to a surge in defaults.

To qualify for this program, borrowers would have to be at least three months behind on their home loans, and would need to owe 90% or more of their home's current value. Investors who do not occupy their homes will face exclusion, as would borrowers who have filed for bankruptcy.

Citigroup Bank announced it is halting foreclosures for borrowers who live in their own homes, have decent incomes and stand a good chance of making lowered mortgage payments. The banking giant also said it is also working to expand the program to include mortgages for which the bank collects payments but does not own.

Additionally, over the next six months, Citigroup Bank plans to reach out to 500,000 homeowners who are not currently behind on their mortgage payments, but who are on the verge of falling behind. This represents about one-third of all the mortgages Citigroup Bank owns.

Citigroup Bank plans to devote a team of 600 salespeople to assist the targeted borrowers by adjusting their rates, reducing principal or increasing the term of the loan.

JPMorgan Chase expanded its mortgage modification program to an estimated $70 billion in loans, which could aid as many as 400,000 customers. The bank has already modified about $40 billion in mortgages, helping 250,000 customers since early 2007.

In late October, a coalition of lenders and consumer advocates asked banking regulators to approve a pilot program that would allow struggling borrowers to pay off, over time, less than they owe—as much as 40% less. Under current rules, any repayment plan has to be for the full amount owed.

In the first proposal on the joint project, the financial services roundtable and the Consumer Federation of America are proposing that certified credit counselors would have evaluated those needing help.

Those who could not pay off their debt under a regular debt management program, which has resulted in the current increase in defaults, would have been placed in one of four repayment plans that would reduce their principal by 10%, 20%, 30% or 40%. Only consumers closest to bankruptcy could have qualified for the biggest reduction.

What should renters do if they receive a foreclosure or eviction notice? Don't panic or stick your head in the sand. Neither action will be helpful says Robert Baker, Education Coordinator at Housing and Credit Counseling Inc. in Kansas.
Robert Baker, http://www.bkforum.com

"Call the sheriff's department first," Baker says. Find out how long the foreclosure process takes. Is it 60 days or 90 days? Then you will have a timeline to work with and time to prepare for the worst-case scenario. Next, get on the Internet. Find out the rental laws in your state. Some states, including California and Illinois, have recently passed legislation giving renters a grace period, ranging from 30 days and up, to stay in a property after it's been sold in foreclosure. Others are considering similar legislation.

The U.S. Department of Housing and Urban Development outlines tenant rights by state on its website.

The lender's name or its lawyer will be on the eviction notice. Contact either one to let them know you are in the property. Find out what your options are. Will the lender let you sign a new lease or is the bank offering some cash assistance for moving out? Do not let the lender bully you into moving out sooner than stated by law.

If you are nervous about negotiating with the lender on your own, contact a local nonprofit housing counseling agency for help. HUD's website lists agencies by state or you can call its toll-free number 1-800-569-4287.

14

MAKE MORE MONEY FROM COMPOUND INTEREST

Do you know how often your lender is compounding interest payments on the debt you owe? Have they disclosed this important piece of information to you? Today it's possible to compound interest monthly, daily, and in the limiting case, *continuously*, meaning that your balance grows by a small amount every instant.

Home and auto loans are compounded monthly. Credit card and consumer loans can be compounded using anyone of the combinations above. Simply put, compounding equates to one dollar ($1) at 24% becomes $1.24. In the next payment cycle, if left unpaid $1.24 at 24% then becomes $1.36 and so on. This is an example of compounded interest on interest.

There are two basic kinds of interest: simple and compound.
Simple interest: If you loaned $300 to a friend for one month and charged her 1% interest ($3) at the end of the month, you would be dealing with simple interest.
Compound interest: With compound interest, the money you borrow becomes the basis of **principal**, and this starts to earn interest on top of principal and interest. If you loaned that same friend $300 for two months but charged her 1% each month until the end of the first and second month, you would be using compound interest. At the end of the first month, she would owe you $303.

At the end of the second month, she would owe you $306.03. At the end of the third month, she would owe you $309.09, and so on. It is near to impossible to get out of compounding when it accumulates on large balances.

If there is not enough money to pay the full amount, the recommendation is to pay the minimum balance, plus the difference for interest charged. This step will reduce the impact that compounding will have on your debt.

Compound interest is what makes credit cards and loans so difficult to pay off. The rules on matters of interest are the same that apply on the increase in your savings account over time; debt is always in the bank's favor—not yours. With some rates as high as 35%, collecting interest on credit card loans can be a lucrative business.
Annenberg Media,
http://www.learner.org/workshops/economics/workshops.html (accessed May 12, 2009).

The concept of compounding interest is something that every person needs to understand. It can keep you poor or increase financial security. Compounding is the number one cause for poverty and financial ruin in America. Consumers get sucked in and rarely ever make it out. Compounding takes away any opportunity for you to thrive. More people in poverty owe their misfortune to the compound interest factor that creates a mountain of debt. The money borrowed is like small change compared to some interest rates that consumers are paying. You never want to borrow $1,000 and owe $1,500 in interest. It is important to keep balances low so that the interest rate does not compound beyond your ability to pay it off in a timely manner. The goal should always be to gain interest, not owe it. Make your money work for you not against you

Compounding based on a $1,000 credit card loan at a 21% interest rate

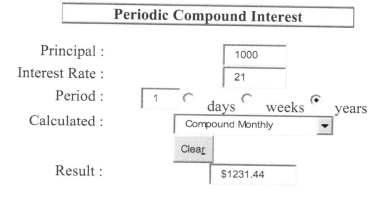

Compounding based on a $25,000 credit card loan at a 21% interest rate

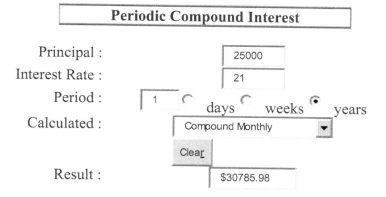

Compounding advantage based on a $25,000 credit card loan at a 14% interest rate

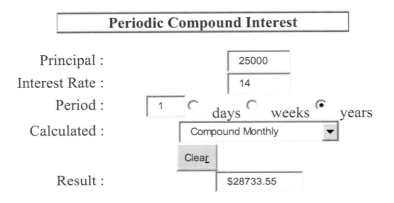

A move from 21% to a 14% decrease in interest rates will yield approximate savings of $2,000 per year.

The minimum monthly payments requested by creditors are normally less than two percent (2%) of the balance on your account. The idea is to lock you in for the long term by requiring such a low payment. As the principal and interest balance compounds, the debt starts to explode.

It is possible to reverse compound debt by adding 10% more to your monthly payment. This reduces the interest amount on your debt that you need to pay. The goal is to reduce interest on debt as quickly as possible, and eventually the extra money will be yours. You can say goodbye to compound debt and hello to compound income.

Compounded debt reduction makes sense, so use it to your advantage. Your goal is to pay the minimum balance requested, and ten percent (10 %) on top of that amount to cover the compound interest cost.

As an example: The minimum balance requested by your creditor is $100 on a $1500 credit card debt and the interest is $80. Pay $100 plus ($80 x 10 % = $8). If you pay $108.00 that extra $8 will reduce the revolving compound interest balance on the monthly charge. By adding more money, you create the "seesaw effect." Over time, **debt decreases and income increases. Reducing the high interest charge is your number one focus.**

After 12 months of consistent payments, compound interest should decline by 50%. Banks are willing to reward customers for consistent payments. Make sure you remind them. I have known rates to change from 30% to 15%. High interest rates are like worms—"They eat your money inside out." Control the interest rate and you win!

You do not have to pay off all your debts to be debt-free. Managing debt by consolidation, compound interest reduction, consistent bill payment, and a common sense money management approach becomes the basis for living debt-free.

The idea is to take baby steps which lead you closer towards lowering debt and creating more income. Americans can maintain their standard of living by good common sense money management and a low debt to income ratio.

Start building your nest egg one transaction at a time. Reducing debt increases the success rate for a stronger financial future. A 50% drop in your credit card interest rate can produce a lot of free cash every month. Most people understand this because it's not only on paper, its hard cold cash. In two years or less, you can turn cash negative into cash positive.

Adjusting your interest rate from 21% to 14% is a great start for a beginner trying to make it out of debt. **If you can save money, you have already made money.**

Let me "show you the money." This example shows the benefit of an adjusted 21% to 14% cost to borrow money. A $25,000 credit card balance with a 7% interest reduction produces the kind of savings illustrated in the calculation below:

$25,000 @21% = 30,785

$25,000 at 14% = 28,733

$2,052 savings

If you were to invest that $2,052 savings each year for three (3) additional years at four percent (4%) you would end up with $8,208 - $8,864 = $656 interest income. I'd rather get $656 than owe that amount. This is how compound interest works for you.

Inputs		
Current Principal:	$	2,052.00
Annual Addition:	$	2,052.00
Years to grow:		3
Interest Rate:		4 %
Compound interest	12	time(s) annually
Make additions at ○ start ● end of each compounding period		
Results		
Future Value:	$	8,863.97

When you put it all together, you have made an eleven percent (11%) return on your money. The 7% drop in your interest rate on the $25,000 credit card debt plus the 4% earned on your investment per the above schedule. Compounding makes sense when debt becomes income.

15

REPAIR DISTRESSED CREDIT – SAVE $100S

Between banks charging higher interest rates and fees for who knows what, and the current economic decline, most Americans have worse credit today than ever before. Be proactive and check your credit scores every twelve months for accuracy. All lending institutions loan money based on credit scoring criteria. Consistent payment cycles are the key to getting better scores.

The three major credit bureau agencies are:

Equifax	Experian	TransUnion
P.O. Box 740241	P.O. Box 2002	P.O. Box 1000
Atlanta, GA 30374	Allen, TX 75013	Chester, PA 19022
1-800-685-1111	1 888 397 3742	1-800-888-4213

TransUnion   EQUIFAX   Experian

Poor	Fair	Good	Excellent
349 - 619	620 - 659	660 - 749	750 - 849

What is Your Credit Score?

Credit scores tell potential lenders everything they need to know about a future customer. Are you a high- or low-risk customer? In other words, your credit score informs lenders if you are making timely payments. The more risk involved, the less likely you will get a loan or decent interest rates.

Did you know that there are many different credit scores? There are an estimated 1,000 being used by lenders and other businesses.

The truth is that there isn't even just one FICO score, although you often hear there is only one "real" score, and it is "the" FICO score. If that is the case, the question is which FICO score is the "real" one?

FICO is not the name of a credit score. It is an acronym for a company: Fair, Isaac Corporation. Fair, Isaac Corporation produces credit scores (note scores is plural, not just one) for lenders and other businesses. Any score from a system developed by Fair, Isaac Corporation is called a FICO score.

While there are generic FICO scores used for all types of lending, as you have discovered, there also are FICO scores for specific types of lending.

There is a FICO score designed for auto lending. There are also FICO scores designed for mortgage lending and insurance purposes. Further, there are FICO scores for specific types of lenders, such as credit unions or traditional banks. Adding to that, there are FICO credit scores created for specific lenders, called custom scores.

Lenders consider your credit score when determining your financial risk. Having a low credit score will put you in a very difficult position to secure a decent loan. Credit scores are calculated using the FICO formula which has a range between 300 and 850. In general, having a credit score of 700 indicates minimal risk. However, the statistical median is 723. The average U.S. score is 693

Your credit score does not take into consideration your salary and savings because your income is not a strong indicator of how likely you are to make payments. Instead of looking at how much money you make, lenders want to see how long you have been dealing with creditors so they can determine how capable you are at managing your payments.

The most important step to repair your credit is by "managing your creditors."

Repairing credit requires that you pay your bills on time. Paying on time will increase your score by 50 points. You can do this as a simple six-month exercise. However, the more credit you apply for in a six-month period the more it will drive down your score. Every new account reduces your score by a 50-point loss. This is how credit scores work until you build a payment history on the new transaction.

Keep paying on your credit balances. Good credit is based on a consistent payment trend. Check your credit data on a regular basis for accuracy and clarity. Consumers need to be aware of a problem before a major purchase. Information on your credit report that is incorrect due to identity theft is a major problem that needs correcting ASAP.

You need to be comfortable that your information is accurate. Get your credit report updates from the official credit rating agencies rather than some internet site. It's cheaper and in some cases free.

Free Annual Consumer Credit Report Act (FACT):
Beginning December 1, 2004, thanks to the federal Fair and Accurate Credit Transactions Act of 2003, (FACT Act), a new program makes free annual consumer credit reports available nationally, simply for the asking.

Your rights under the FACT Act are in addition to any rights you may already have to a free consumer credit report under existing law. Under the FACT Act program, you are entitled to one free consumer credit report annually from each of the three nationwide consumer credit reporting agencies: Equifax, Experian, and Trans-Union.

Challenge yourself by setting a goal for the credit score of your choice, and then pursue it!

Bad credit scores can be improved. Improving your credit score is not as difficult as most believe. The most important thing is to keep on paying your bills no matter what. Consistency is the measurement used to improve and build your credit score.

Direct payments are one of the most common methods used to make sure that creditors receive payment consistently and on time. Make this request through your local bank. You may set an amount that you want to pay monthly. If you have spare cash in a particular month, you can pay more by sending in a separate check.

On-time payment saves you $100s every month in late fees and penalties. A consistent bill payment pattern is your road to getting better credit scores. It is possible to reach your credit score goal.

Sometimes credit card companies may be working from old and incorrect data. This data may belong to someone else, which will cost you hundreds of dollars extra in fees, as merchants see you in the higher risk category. In many instances this is inaccurate; you just need to get it corrected. Anything on your report that appears to be incorrect, it probably is. Do not hesitate; question unreasonable terms and discrepancies on your report. Why pay more when you are not at fault!

Bad information affects your overall credit score. When merchants send bad data to the credit agencies, it becomes a matter of rubbish in rubbish out. IMPORTANT—check all statements as credit card companies are increasing your rate without notice. This happens as they secretly assess your risk level. Apparently, if you have fair or not-so-good credit scores, you are going to be affected. Therefore, it should be your highest priority to periodically check your credit report at least twice per year.

Here is something you may not know! VANTAGE SCORE SCALE

This score scale approximates your number to a letter grade. You now will have clear insight into how lenders using this score will view your creditworthiness.

901 - 990: A - top 11% of the population
801 - 900: B - top 40% of the population
701 - 800: C - top 60% of the population
601 - 700: D - lower 40% of the population
501 - 600: F - lowest 19% of the population

The grade of D, represents the bottom 40% of all consumers. A previous bankruptcy on file, two charged-off accounts and 30 days past due on one account. The past due account is also over its credit limit. That is the conditions for the letter grade D.

Bankruptcies stay on a credit report for 7-10 years and delinquencies remain for 7 years.

However, you can take some actions to improve the credit score.
1. Pay the past due amount on the delinquent account.
2. Reduce the balances on the revolving accounts
3. Continue to pay all accounts on time and allow the passage of time to reduce the effects of previous delinquencies. It is so important to understand how you are being measured for credit purposes.

16

SQUEEZE MORE MONEY FROM CAR LOANS AND WARRANTIES

The best way to save on car loan costs is to go through a credit union. Credit unions offer rates that beat most Main Street lenders. You can save 3% over the traditional loan.

Car payments that go beyond three years are not a good use of your money. Normally after three years you enter the period when more maintenance and repair is required. It makes sense not to get caught making car payments and incurring repairs costs at the same time.

Car dealers are good at convincing buyers to commit by stretching payments five years out to make it feel affordable. What appears to be a good short-term deal ends up costing much more at the end. This is good for the dealer but bad for you the customer. Remember, this is a buyer's market—you call the shots. Be tough, be open-minded and ask the right questions. Learn to play the game and win.

Buying an extended car warranty with all the coverage restrictions is not worth your time and money. Cars have a shorter life-span than they did ten years ago. Here are some strategies to consider when buying a car. No extended warranty is needed after the basic manufacturer's warranty expires. Why pay extra for peace-of-mind when you can get a good mechanic at the fraction of the cost? There are three costs that make warranties a bad choice: the warranty payments, out-of-pocket costs, and items not covered under the warranty.

Be realistic, be reasonable, but don't be a sucker. Salespeople are desperate for your businesses. Don't show that you are desperate for theirs. Your costs will be higher. If you give them a bone, they will turn it into meat! Never fall for the hard sell.

When thinking about warranties on used cars, rethink. The warranty at that point is a waste of your money. It's a minefield to figure out what is supposed to be covered under the warranty agreement, as everything that can go wrong will go wrong. The alternative cost saver is to take the vehicle to a local mechanic, negotiate the job, and buy your own parts. It will be cheaper than the warranty premiums and additional out-of-pocket expenses.

Your objective as a buyer is to pay the lowest cost and get the best value. The seller wins by making a profit on the sale, and you win by getting the best deal at the most competitive cost. It's your money—don't be influenced into spending more than you need to.

Dealers mark up the prices on cars to reflect higher margins. Some dealers' marked-up rates are in excess of 60% on manufacturer's cost. There is potential for you to reduce your cost by up to sixty percent (60%).

Dealers always come out ahead. If you take out the overhead, commission and incidentals from the sale price the dealer comes out ahead by around 20%.Consumers can negotiate another 5% discount off the dealers' profit.

Example: $20,000.00 sales price, minus 5% of dealers profit = $1,000.00 savings.

If all fails, tell the salesperson that you need to get another quote. Another technique is to keep looking over the street at the competition while the sales person is talking. You will be surprised how the appearance of distraction will work in your favor.

Most consumer goods come with a 1-year manufacturer's warranty from the date of purchase. Therefore, additional one-year coverage is not practical on a standard product like computers and printers. The seller might recommend this only to get a bigger commission. Consumer items and appliances like computers and washing machines last beyond three years. Warranties for the most part cover only parts and you get stuck with the labor. It makes sense to save the warranty payments and put it towards a newer model when that current one goes bad.

There is no value in a warranty on consumer items in the second and third years. Most items last for three years anyway. Then they go bad and the warranty runs out. What just happened? You paid for the item, a warranty that just ran out, and now you need to spring more money for a replacement. That does not make any sense!

17

THE COMMON SENSE IN BANKING

It does not make sense to jump banks when there is a problem with your account. Work it out with the branch manager. Maintaining some kind of history at a bank has its advantages. Your bank knows you and they understand your account history. Your current bank is easier to deal with than a bank that knows nothing about you. Changing banks can also affect your credit score. Banks want to keep your business. I have never seen a bank say they don't need your business. Banks are more than willing to work with you to reduce or eliminate bank charges and annoying fees. Waiving fees is very common. Just ask. You will never know until you ask.

Banks are always making concessions to compete in the market for new or repeat business. At least once every year you need to sit down and speak to your banker. They are always creating new consumer items that have great money savings features. Speak to your banker when you are having financial difficulty. Have these conversations way before things get out of control.

Fees charged on small business accounts upon request can go away. Your bank is not obligated to tell you what products will save you money. The key is to ask. If your account is not in good standing, don't let that prevent you from asking for a better deal. If you ask, they will most likely say yes, and if you don't ask, you will never know.

Save On Overdraft Charges

There are so many overdraft policies designed by banks to make you pay. Instead of incurring an insufficient-funds fee, I encourage account holders to get an overdraft reserve for free. Banks will arrange a reserve on your account. If you have a payment that is greater than your current balance, the reserve covers you. The only requirement is that you pay the reserve balance in thirty days. This will prevent the additional cost of using the reserve beyond 30 days. An overdraft reserve makes sense because it saves you money.

High Daily Maximums: According to reports from the Consumer Federation of America (CFA) only 35% of major banks set daily maximum for the number of overdraft transactions you can conduct. Unfortunately, most of those limits are high.

Adding to the problem, many banks use a tiered overdraft system that escalates charges for subsequent overdrafts. My bank charges $25 for the first overdraft offense and $32 for other subsequent charges. There is a way out if your account is in good standing. The bank will waive the overdraft fee once every calendar year as a complimentary good faith gesture. That in itself is an average savings of $28.00.

Save on ATM Fees

Debit and ATM Cushions: Debit-card use triggers 46% of all overdrafts, according to the Center for Responsible Lending. "They allow the debits to go through, instead of rejecting them."

Save on Car Insurance Costs

Car insurance is one of the most overlooked and misunderstood expenses by customers—even during times of tight budget and monetary constraints.

The fact is that car insurance providers are increasing their premiums annually. When was the last time you shopped for car insurance? Surf the market for the best premium possible. It is a competitive market out there. Your bank is a great resource to find the best insurers at competitive rates. Tip: share your insurance policy to get an apple-to-apples comparison, and then choose.

Shop around. Check rates online at InsWeb.com, call companies, and consult an agent through the <u>Independent Insurance Agents & Brokers of America</u>. Rates vary depending on a company's operating expenses, history of claims and formulas for setting premiums. Check a company's financial status and consumer record. The last thing you need is to go cheap and then find it's all but impossible to file a claim.

Your bank is a great resource for car loans and other services. Leverage the relationship and save.

Small, fuel-efficient vehicles are flying off the lots faster than some dealers can stock them—and what a turnaround this is in the automotive industry.

In May 2008, the Ford F-150 truck, which had been the best-selling vehicle in the country for two decades, lost its title to the fuel-sipping Honda Civic.

Tip: plan for smaller fuel-efficient cars in the future. Gas prices are just waiting for another opportunity to go up.

Detroit has responded by putting more emphasis on smaller vehicles, such as the Ford Focus and the Chevy Malibu, but Toyota, Honda and Nissan continue to dominate when it comes to fuel efficiency.

Here are the top 10 of the 2008 model year:

1. Toyota Prius
2. Honda Civic Hybrid
3. Toyota Camry Hybrid
4. Toyota Yaris
5. Honda Fit
6. Toyota Corolla
7. Mini Cooper
8. Hyundai Accent/Kia Rio
9. Honda Civic
10. Nissan Versa

Top deals now, according to TrueCar.com, include the Mercury Mountaineer SUV at a discount of 19.3%; the Porsche 911 (-10.6%) at the high end; Toyota's Camry Hybrid (-9.4%) and Highlander Hybrid (-8.7%); and among compacts the Kia Optima (-30.8%) and Ford Fusion (-23.5%).

18

SQUEEZE THE CENTS FROM YOUR TAXES

Get more money from your taxes by using credits to reduce your liability. States did not pay out 2008 homestead rebates this year, and will not issue them next year, even though you qualify for it. You need to find other sources to "squeeze the cents out of taxes." A first time homebuyer qualifies for a refundable $8,000 tax credit. Therefore, if you have a federal income tax liability of $5,000 without the tax credit you would owe the IRS $5 000.00 for 2009. Suppose now that the taxpayer qualified for the $8,000 homebuyer tax credit. As a result, the taxpayer would receive a check for $3,000 ($8,000 minus the $5,000 owed).

A tax credit is a dollar-for-dollar reduction in what you owe. That means that a taxpayer who owes $8,000 in income taxes and who receives an $8,000 tax credit would owe nothing to the IRS.

If you die in 2009, your estate will be exempt from federal tax requirements. Your survivors still need to complete the paperwork for tax purposes. This is a major financial relief for those that have lost loved ones.

The required minimum withdrawal from IRAs has been suspended for 2009 ONLY. This will give investors and those planning to retire or retired some extra time to recover from their most recent losses fueled by the current economic crisis. It's not always about taking money, stupid. Uncle Sam just did something that makes sense!

File your taxes if you are unemployed or if you have lost your home.

Your tax bill is likely to be lower and you could be due for a larger refund. Look for tax amnesty opportunities through your state government. You might find yourself eligible for a broad range of credits that you didn't qualify for before. Among them: the earned income credit, education credits and the recovery rebate credit.

The earned income tax credit boosts take-home pay. It provides an incentive to work. The maximum income limit is $41,646. That declines based on filing status and the number of children in the household. The maximum credit for 2008 is $4,824, up from $4,716 in 2007.

Credits that save Taxpayers Money

These credits can increase a refund or reduce a tax bill. Usually, credits can only lower a tax liability to zero. But some credits, such as the EITC, the child tax credit, the recovery rebate credit and the first-time homebuyer credit, are refundable — in other words, they can make the difference between a balance due and a refund.

What if I lose my home through foreclosure?

Under the Mortgage Forgiveness Debt Relief Act of 2007, taxpayers generally can exclude income from the discharge of debt on their principal residence or mortgage restructuring. This exception does not apply to second homes or vacation homes. In some cases, you may be able to file an amended tax return for previous tax years

What if I file for bankruptcy protection?

Debts discharged through bankruptcy are not taxable income. If you are an individual debtor who files for bankruptcy under chapter 7 of the Bankruptcy Code, a separate "estate" is created consisting of property that belonged to you before the filing date. This bankruptcy estate is a new taxable entity, completely separate from you as an individual taxpayer. Please note, however, that some tax debts are not dischargeable in a bankruptcy action.

What if my 401(k) drops in value?

You can claim a capital loss when you receive a distribution that had previously been taxed

What if I can't pay my taxes?

The IRS may be able to provide some relief such as a short-term extension to pay, an installment agreement or an offer in compromise. In some cases, the agency may be able to waive penalties. However, the agency is unable to waive interest charges which accrue on unpaid tax bills

Tax Credit

Under the American Recovery and Reinvestment Act, more people will qualify for the **American Opportunity Tax Credit**, which modifies the existing Hope Credit for tax years 2009 and 2010 and makes the Hope Credit available to a broader range of taxpayers, including many with higher incomes and those who do not owe tax.

The new credit also adds required course materials to the list of qualifying expenses and allows the credit to be claimed for four post-secondary education years, instead of two years.

Find a tax consultant that is willing to fight for every dollar that you are entitled to under the tax law. Good tax accountants will turn over every tax code in an effort to get you the most on your return. Most consumers get a tax accountant that does the bare minimum. There is no value or benefit to you if your tax person is not willing to do the research and keep current.

Who can afford to lose $1,000s in tax rebates due to a tax preparer's mistake? The solution is to keep an eye on your tax return as detected mistakes equals' additional rebate dollars.

The flaw in tax preparation is in the tax preparer's approach. Tax preparers are doing multiple returns at any given time. Tax preparation becomes a matter of quantity over quality. There is **no guarantee that your return will get special attention or preferential treatment over and above normal review and entitlements**. If you allow it, your tax preparation becomes another return on the production line.

To prevent this production line mentality and the lack of attention to detail on your particular return, take the time to understand what your tax preparer is doing on your behalf. Get involved. Make sure that you advocate for every red cent of your entitlement. If you do not want to interfere with your preparer, shop for a new tax accountant. You will be amazed at the savings that a new pair of eyes can generate for you.

Your entitlements can be greater and more extensive than what your tax preparer is settling for. Tax preparers need to earn their fee.

Cash in on Deferred Billing

Buy now pay later with no interest payments for ninety days sounds like a great way to keep your cost down. The dark side of this deal is the interest charge kicks in and you're not prepared for it. You've just been sucked in.

Working from a deferred interest payment program allows you to enjoy the short-term benefits of zero payments. However, your payment will sky rocket from easy to pay to hard to keep up with.

Buying now and paying later at zero interest only makes sense if you can reduce your risk. If you are willing to pay a smaller amount than you normally would during the ninety-day period, using this strategy makes the deferred option a benefit in two ways: One, it takes away the shock associated with having to pay out more money that is not part of your budget. Two, it saves you money later and reduces the compound interest component of the deferred charge.

The compound interest on the deferred charge can drop by twenty percent (20%). See example 1 and 2 below:

Example 1
Deferred period – 90 days
Deferred loan - $500
Interest rate – 25%
Cost at thirty-day period (510.42)
Cost at sixty-day period (521.05)
Cost at ninety-day period (531.91)

Example 2
Loan - $500
Interest rate – 25%
Monthly payment - $50
Cost at thirty-day period (510.42)
Cost at sixty-day period (480.86)

Cost at ninety-day period (439.83)

After the ninety-day deferred payment period is over, your cost will start at $531.91 versus $439.83 if you were paying the minimum amount of $50 per month. Example 2 saves you 20%. By far example two saves money. It makes sense to pay a bit extra on the front-end and save more on the back-end. This is a common sense money tip.

Another tip is to pay a small sum directly from your account every month during the ninety-day period. If you do not see it, you will not feel it. This tip reduces the stress and worry about paying for the amount outstanding at the end. Buy on your terms! Some deferred payments may affect your taxable income. You are enjoying the benefit of an item that no tax has been collected on. Think about deferred sales or use tax as a starting point.

19

EXERCISE YOUR RIGHT TO NEGOTIATE
SAVE $1,000S

Never settle for the first offer! That is the first rule in negotiation. The second rule is doing your research. The third rule is, never leave money on the table. Consumers leave so much money on the table because they did not understand how further they could have gone to drive a better deal. It pays to negotiate. Go all the way.

There is a well known story of a man that went to a car dealership and wanted to buy a car. The buyer was not comfortable with the price and the terms. He started negotiating with little success. After numerous attempts the dealer would not budge. Suddenly the buyer had an idea. He said to the dealer, "Would you accept a five-hundred dollar down payment?" And he suggested paying $250 monthly over the term. While he was saying that he started nodding his head in acknowledgement to the dealer. After a while, the dealer started to nod his head also, and the deal closed. It's all about the results. You can be as creative as you want by thinking outside the box.

The reality is that buyers need to put their requirements on the table so that sellers know what your terms are up front. This becomes your starting point. It's very simple—tell them what you have, then ask them to work with you. No need for surprises or an "ace up the sleeve." **Whoever has the cash has the power to negotiate**! This is a buyer's market. You need to make the deal. Too often the consumer gives in to the seller without getting the best deal possible.

Exercise your right to negotiate or walk away. You need to decide if this is going to be a "deal or no deal."

Timing is everything when you want the best results. Timing your negotiation can yield many benefits and can be conducted in a variety of ways. Knowledge is power in today's market-driven economy. Understanding the seller's areas of vulnerability include "meeting monthly sales targets." This is a good place to start.

Sellers need to make the sale as the amount of their monthly commission checks depends on it. Your best option is to buy at the end of the month. This is a common strategy, the reason being that sellers have to close accounts and commissions need to be calculated. The buyer can put the pressure on sellers at this point of vulnerability. Using this information to time your purchase can result in $1,000s of dollars in savings.

Educate yourself by going to competitors to get an idea of their cost, and then go to the supplier that you intend to purchase from, tell them that the competition has the same product at a cost less than what they are offering. Then ask the question, are you willing to match and beat the competitor's offer? Big merchants encourage consumers to come with an offer that is an apple-to-apple comparison. If it beats their price they will match or beat it to get the business. This is a very common practice. So if you think you can't do it, think again.

You will be amazed at the respect you will get when you appear to be informed and knowledgeable. Sellers will accept a lower price to make the sale.

Always remember when engaging in negotiations, the seller needs to make a profit. If you try to negotiate for you to win and the supplier to lose this will not be acceptable, and the deal will fall apart. I have seen this happen so many times. Once you show that you are unreasonable, sellers will not entertain any further requests from you, even if it is reasonable. There is a point of no return.

Negotiating 101

The two types of negotiation that are most commonly used are haggling and strategic.

Haggling:

Haggling is a basic communication style that requires no preparation planning or strategic thinking.

Consider Merchant A is selling a product for $10. In a haggling situation, the buyer B will inform the seller that he is offering $5. If the seller holds strong on the price, the outcome for this request becomes a deadlocked transaction. This style of communication results in a take it or leave it attitude.

Haggling is beneficial in transactions that are low in value, and are immediately available. The final agreement between both parties ends at the point when a price is accepted and an exchanged of goods for cash takes place.

There is no value beyond price. Values such as performance, and warranty claims are non-existent under a haggling scenario. When a problem exists with the product, there is no way out to get monetary restitution. It is easier to exchange these items only.

Haggling is the most basic form of communication that yields the most limited financial results and the lowest commitment to quality and performance.

Yard sale is a perfect environment where haggling can flourish when low cost items are being sought. Buyers place a low value on these items because they are convenient.

Items bought using the haggling style of negotiation do not have an expected value beyond their intended use. Most people prefer haggling because it is simple and requires no effort or intelligence, just a little influence.

Strategic:

Negotiation is the skillful art of plotting through a series of thoroughly planned discussions. Negotiation is all about "market intelligence." Either you have it or you don't. Building and using market intelligence will get the results that you need.

Negotiating the best deal possible is only limited to your ability to effectively negotiate.

Negotiation is the most intelligent form of communicating your position through a well-constructed dialogue of facts, resulting in an exchange of cash for services. Negotiation is a discipline that yields the highest results if executed timely, correctly and with precision.

The goal of negotiations is to get the best value at the lowest cost over the longest period. Harnessing this skill will be beneficial to those who either learn it or possess it, especially in periods of economic downturns when money is tight and every penny counts.

"To defeat an opponent you must first think like an opponent." Master negotiators are always thinking about what's in it for the other party. There has to be a clear benefit for the other party to seriously negotiate.

There is no mystique when it comes to negotiation. Creative thinking is the only criteria that you need to acquire. Sellers are more than willing to slash costs if you do your homework. Before you take a vacation, you will plan where and when you are going. How much you have to spend and how long you will be staying.

As an example, let's look at the clothing industry. A little research on what clothing merchants are doing in their respective markets goes a long way towards sharpening your negotiation skills and can yield huge financial benefits. Knowing who the major players are is a powerful information tool for negotiating price.

Most clothing companies produce more than they can sell. What do they do with the excess? They either discount it or sell to a wholesaler that sells brand name items at a reduced price. So why go to a brand name store when you can get the same item for 50% off? Now there is an opportunity to decrease clothing costs by 50%.

The same principle applies when purchasing a car. The following are common sense questions that you need to know the answer to:
1. Is the manufacturer offering discounts and incentives to the dealer that needs to pass through to you the buyer?
2. Has this discount passed on to you as the end user through a lower retail asking price?

Forget about the mail-in rebate offers. You need to get the benefit of the price reduction now, rather than later. Serious dealers will discount the car price to a level that is within their margin so that they can make a reasonable profit on the sale. You, as the consumer have to learn how to time your approach and wait for the results. Do not be too quick to say yes!

The consumer always receives a bad deal over the term of the car-financing period when they say yes too quickly. Successful negotiation requires patience. You can get a better deal that is over a shorter term and at a cheaper price if you can harness this discipline. Many sales people will admit that consumers would have paid less and saved more had they not shown signs of excitement.

A five-year financing deal is a waste of money. Long-term deals like that are a loss to you and a gain to the finance company. Don't sign up for long-term commitments that will cause a negative impact on your finances. Long term financing on car loans eliminates your long-term cash flow possibilities. Get rid of the excess costs and save over the shortest period.

Negotiate from a point of strength. This is a consumer market. Sound market intelligence will give you the edge needed to get the best deal at the lowest cost. Use competitors if you need to leverage your position.

It's true that you're not going to win in negotiating if you don't think about the other party. You must be willing to make the offer worthwhile for them. However, it doesn't mean you play to tie.

Exercise your right to negotiate a better service agreement that provides some security in the event your purchase does not function as expected. Wring the cents out of service contracts and save thousands of dollars. When that item you purchased is not working, you lose money. Time is money. Get a service deal that includes replacement options or a money-back guarantee without the tricks. If they cannot replace it, don't waste your time and money. Merchants need to stand behind their product.

Good Loan-Bad Loan

We all have to borrow money at some point. How much do you want and what price are you eager to pay? Lenders have no limit. They charge whatever someone desperate enough for money will pay. **This economic crisis has ruined many folks with good credit.**

Consumers with good credit turned bad struggle to get ahead and enjoy the basic comforts that loans offer when cash is not available. Desperate times call for desperate measures. Desperate consumers continue to go for the high interest rate loans due to restrictions placed on them by bad credit scores and other factors.

A high interest loan for many consumers is the only option in this depressed economic climate. Loan companies that charge exuberant rates are loan sharks. Loan sharking is an all too familiar practice. It's a take it or leave it mentality. The Gen X population like Jane for the first time in their lives is in an unfamiliar environment. This environment is far different from the years of excess and plenty that has become a way of life for many Americans.

To have the advantage over a loan shark, you must put up some collateral. An example would be companies that give you cash for your title. If you do not pay, you lose your asset. This is a cheaper way to get that needed cash quicker and with no risk to the lender.

Loan sharks charge high rates because of the risk they assume. It is an understanding in that industry that the lenders money is at risk. There is a 70% chance the lender will not get their money back in a timely manner. Therefore, the maximum legal interest charge covers the loan in the shortest period.

Reduce that risk and you will beat them at their own game. Find something to collateralize your loan and you can come out ahead when borrowing from these sources.

It's your money and your future. Don't let loan sharks take advantage of your misfortune.

Just Enough Insurance Coverage Required

Repeat after me: *Insurance is not an investment.* If you have universal whole life, it is time to switch to term insurance. Term insurance is cheaper and will save you up to 60% in this challenging economy. Use that difference in cost to pay down on debt or add to savings.

A term policy is the best life coverage at a reasonable cost. On the death of the insured, it pays the face amount of the policy to the named beneficiary. You can buy term for periods of one year to 30 years. Whole life insurance, on the other hand, combines a term policy with an investment component. You don't need it. The investment could be in bonds and money-market instruments or stocks. The policy builds cash value that you can borrow against in the future. The three most common types of whole life insurance are traditional whole life policies, universal and variable. With both whole life and term, you can lock in the same monthly payment over the life of the policy.

Whole life insurance is expensive: You're paying not only for insurance but also for the cash back or investment portion. That extra cost might almost be worth it if these policies were a good investment vehicle.

Nevertheless, insurance agents like to call these policies retirement plans, emphasizing the "forced savings" element. However, the inherent result is to get consumers to part with their money by paying higher premiums each month for coverage they do not need.

The homeowner's insurance market is very competitive right now. There is no reason why in this distressful-economic climate those prices should be up. On the contrary, insurance cost should be consistently in lock step with the market, which is trending downwards. Homeowner's insurance is a minefield to navigate. However, there are still great insurance rates available for the picking.

In times of tight budgets and less money, consumers are more willing to cut corners, which can be devastating in the event of an insurance-related emergency.

Accidents will happen, which will result in a claim, a claim for which you may find you have no coverage. There is no need for you to go that route. Shop around for the best rates available and shave your current insurance cost.

There is a better way to save on insurance costs rather than not paying your premiums. Rates are competitive in your area **especially** from providers who are not household names. They are just as reputable and provide same level of service. You can determine this by comparing the policy coverage.

Use your current insurance policy as the base to compare and get better rates. You will be surprised at what a second opinion can do to improve your coverage and shave $100s off your homeowners' insurance bill. Remember, everything is negotiable. Don't leave your money on the table.

<u>20</u>

THRIVE

A Rewarding Experience

Some Americans may be able to undertake great cost-cutting efforts during this recession and recovery that is sure to make a big impact on their spend reduction efforts. Others may only be able to do small things in a great way. Either way, the idea is to build financial security, reduce risk and thrive.

At this stage of the book, you should be feeling a renewed sense of **<u>financial empowerment</u>**. You have now discovered what many smart people have known for decades. Common people manage money better when a Common Sense approach to personal finances becomes the basis of their shopping experience. Common sense money management is an invaluable life skill. Making the transition from being loaded with debt to managing debt effectively is a great achievement.

Power-Shoppers Buy More and Pay Less!

Power-shoppers are always on the lookout for quality at a fair price. This is how they shop. It does not matter if they have a lot or a little money. Power-shoppers understand the value of a dollar, and they know when they are being taken on price. A handbag cost $60 over a year ago. Today you can get the same bag 75% off. What has changed? The seller is willing to take a lower profit margin to make the sale. Power-shoppers have known this all along. Consumers are just finding this out. They have been overpaying and it's all profit for the merchant. Power-shoppers face resentment because the perception about them says everything cheap! Now that the economy has turned over, **everyone** is power-shopping. Power-shoppers have come back to save the day. They are truly the pistons that will drive the economic recovery. Power-shopping is in, and it's also fashionable.

As merchants offer between 25-75% discounts on consumer goods, they desperately need buyers to take the goods off their shelves. This economic slowdown has given consumers insight into the inflated pricing mechanism used by merchants. When the economy turns around and prices start to inflate, remember you are a "Power-Shopper."

Many retail stores are failing because of the erosion of their traditional customer base. They did not appeal to the power-shopping group. Now they want to get anyone just to come in the door to shop.

Consumers were embarrassed in the past to power-shop; they felt that it was beneath them to go through the discount rack or a clearance center. This economic climate has educated consumers on the value of being a bargain hunter. It is currently un-American to be anything else. Today, everybody is a power-shopper. Power-shoppers are ramping up as the next big wave in consumer spending to boost the American economy way into the 21st century. The Chinese have been doing this for centuries. Way to go America!

Clearance outlets are dotted across America. These outlets are clearance houses for the major brand name stores that have goods in inventory, which is less than perfect but still very good. This is where the power shoppers go for bargains. Main Street merchants are catching up by appealing to this section of the economy.

Many home and general merchandise franchises have clearance outlets throughout the United States. These clearance centers sell items that you would normally find in any of the retail stores. Look for them in your local area. Pay up to 70% off retail. The catch is that all the items sold are a little less than perfect.

The list below is representative of what is available to help you save, when money is tight and quality is still high on your list.

Target Coupons	**Target's Online Clearance Outlet** Save up to 75% instantly (while quantities last)	Valid Anytime
Overstock Coupons	**Overstock's Online Clearance Outlet** Save up to 80% instantly (while quantities last)	Valid Anytime
Coupons	**Overstock's Steals of the Week** Save up to 80% instantly	Valid Anytime
Kohls Coupons	**Kohls.com's Clearance** Save up to 80% instantly	Valid Anytime
Sears Coupons	**Sears' Online Clearance Outlet** Save up to 70% instantly (while quantities last)	Valid Anytime
Home Depot Coupons	**HomeDepot.com's Special Values** Save up to 40% instantly	Valid Anytime
Coupons	**HomeDepot.com's Promotional Sale Center** Save up to $250 instantly	Valid Anytime
Linens N Things Coupons	**Linens & Things' Online Clearance Outlet** Save up to 75% instantly (while quantities last)	Valid Anytime
Joann.com Coupons	**Joann.com's Online Clearance Sale** Save up to 60% instantly (while quantities last)	Valid Anytime

Coupons	**Amazon Outlet's Home Decor Sale** Save up to 50% instantly (Fridays only)	Valid Anytime
Wal-Mart Coupons	**Wal-Mart's Online Home & Garden Clearance Outlet** Save up to 45% instantly	Valid Anytime
Brookstone Coupons	**Brookstone's Online Clearance Outlet** Save up to 60% instantly (while quantities last)	Valid Anytime
ShopNBC Coupons	**ShopNBC.com's Sample Sale** Save up to 70% instantly (while quantities last)	Valid Anytime
Coupons	**Art.com's Online Clearance Gallery** Save up to 75% instantly (while quantities last)	Valid Anytime
Coupons	**Lenox's Online Clearance Outlet** Save up to 75% instantly (while quantities last)	Valid Anytime
LL Bean Coupons	**LLBean.com's Sale** Save up to 55% Instantly	Valid Anytime
Lamps Plus Coupons	**Lamp's Plus Online Clearance Outlet** Save up to 70% instantly (while quantities last)	Valid Anytime
Solutions Catalog Coupons	**Solutions Catalog's Online Clearance Outlet** Save up to 59% instantly	Valid Anytime

A better life awaits all of us as we transition through these tough times and look forward to the best days ever.

To benefit from the good times that are ahead, one has to make the necessary adjustments now. Use your resources wisely, whether they are material possessions, friends, and/or family. Cherish them and they will enrich your life when you need it most.

Entrepreneurs are springing up in all sorts of industries, and in many cases are achieving success. Take Iris Chau and Stephen Chen. Both come from the finance industry.

After the Wall Street meltdown cost them their jobs, they took advantage of an opportunity to combine their skills and start a new business transforming old tires into environmentally friendly recycled shoes. Green Soul Shoes has sold thousands of pairs of sustainable footwear, and with each pair sold; they donate another pair to kids in developing countries. This company would not exist if not for the mass layoffs that led the founders to try something new.

Thousands of laid-off workers are also putting their free time to good use. Nonprofits across the country are reporting a swell in volunteers. At a time of great need, many Americans are taking advantage of their unexpected freedom by getting involved in their communities - from serving as youth mentors to providing the work force needed for renovating community parks and schools.

Layaway Makes a Giant Comeback

In the past, there was a novel way of buying things called "layaway." If you did not have the cash, you could lay it away. The concept is simple: You ask the store to set your item aside, and then make payments until the item is paid in full. The payment period on layaway is normally thirty days. I know this method must be shocking to many since delayed gratification is a foreign concept. As credit became easier, layaway was put to rest. With the way things are with the economy, there is a full blown return to delayed gratification. Layaway makes a comeback.

(Boston Globe) After pulling back on layaway programs for years, retailers are touting the service as a financially perceptive way to buy products Already, many cash-poor and credit-strapped shoppers are responding by flocking to layaway counters at stores and using online options such as **eLayaway.com.**

"The response has just been tremendous," said Tom Aiello, a spokesperson at Kmart, which is running a national holiday ad campaign for its layaway service. "We know for a fact it's a big increase over . . . last year."

What is happening to credit card companies? They are getting body slammed into the ground with rising defaults, thus they have turned to restricting credit on many customers. Customers who are not under consideration for prime lending status can now forget about $20,000 credit lines. Even prime borrowers are seeing their limits lowered. Make no mistake—this upsurge in layaway is simply a manifestation of the desire to still shop, no matter what. "People are looking for ways to buy the things with non-credit based options," said Michael Bilello, senior vice president of business development at eLayaway.com. "The lend-and-spend boom is over."

Consignment Makes Sense

For all those unused items that have a cash value in your basement, there is another cash option called "Consignment."

Provided below is a sample of a <u>consignment contract</u>. You will find it to be a beneficial resource to help you sell those unused items in your basement.

Merchandise tags will show the first three letters of your last name and an account number, along with a description of the item and price.

The bar code information enables the sold tags to be scanned and credited to your account. A complete list of the items you are consigning. Please allow several days for our staff to process your items and display them on the sale floor. You may pick up items that we chose not to sell within 10 days (from the date you delivered them to us).

PERCENTAGE OF SELLING PRICE PAID TO YOU:
40% of the selling price for clothing and accessories
50% of the selling price for household items
50% of the selling price for furniture items fewer than 300.00 (for higher priced items the percentage paid to you may increase up to 65%) All furniture pricing is determined before you leave the store

COLLECTING YOUR MONEY
At the end of the consignment period, 60 days, you may come for a check and a print-out of the items sold. One exception is that you may collect money after 14 business days if your furniture has sold

REDUCTION OF PRICE AND LENGTH OF CONSIGNMENT CONTRACT:
Merchandise will be kept for 60 days. All unsold items will be reduced by 20% after 30 days

UNSOLD ITEMS:
At the end of the 60-day consignment period, ALL UNSOLD items must be picked up within 7 days. The items will be on the sales floor and you will have to retrieve them. We will assist you to identify your UNSOLD items by the information on the tag. If you choose not to reclaim the unsold items, we will automatically donate them to a not for profit organization of our choice.

21

THE BOTTOM LINE

American consumers will only buy if the price is right. That is the bottom line. Manufactures and service providers need to come up with ways to lower their cost to the consumer so that they can sell more products, compete for our dollars and thrive. There are no winners and losers. Everyone benefits.

Having a healthy bottom line is the difference between surviving and thriving. The answer lies partly in the obvious labor and benefits reduction. Beyond that, there is value analysis, taking out cost redundancies, tightening the supply chain, consolidating the supplier base, renegotiating longer contract terms for price reductions, realigning core operations, doing more with less, demand management, strategic alignment of services, speed to market delivery and execution, perceived value, and the list goes on.

Small family-owned and individually operated business enterprises are the growth engine for this economy. That is an undisputed fact. As business, owners start to feel the effects of the economic crisis and a shrinking pool of buyers in the market, activating cost reductions in the quickest possible timeframe will yield the best results in terms of shaving the cost from internal operations and keeping a strong customer base. The idea is to be lean, not mean, to the detriment of your operation's effectiveness and competitiveness. This is the bottom line.

Costs associated with raw materials, overhead and labor are the easiest to reduce. Inventory is cheap as there are fewer orders flowing through the system. The key is to wind down the high cost inventory, secure lower-cost, high-quality inventory and pass the savings to the end user through lower prices. Lower operating costs increases the competitive edge needed to thrive, in a shrinking market.

Value analysis looks at what tools are necessary to give you the edge needed to thrive from a business perspective. Shrinking design costs and methods of production can help. What value does your current list of suppliers add to the supply chain? They should be bringing you new ideas and value propositions to enhance your end product. The value they bring is the value you deliver. Many business entities have been using the same supplier for years these relationships are based on a strong and developed network. Today that is not a good enough reason to keep doing business with them. Key suppliers need to work harder and smarter with you on creative value. Adding programs to drive out cost and save you and your customers money is the bottom line.

The following are examples to illustrate the power of value analysis. UPS has asked pilots to taxi with one engine when possible, and it is experimenting with a type of landing during which engines are idle. The latter measure alone could save up to 70 gallons of fuel per flight. UPS have begun using so-called telematics technology to track more than 200 pieces of data, including speed, oil pressure, and even the number of times a truck goes in reverse. That helped drivers reduce engine idling by 24 minutes per day, saving $188 per driver.

Cutting fuel costs is one thing; building a finance business is another. UPS's figures loans will average around $150,000, and anticipates one or two defaults for every 100 loans issued. "UPS does well with its cash flow, so they have some money they can use [for loans]," says Penn State's Coyle. "But it's a little risky in today's market." UPS has offered such financing to customers over the past decade, but much of the lending was government-backed.

One of its trial customers is Pedors, a $2 million Marietta (Ga.) importer of orthopedic shoes. Along with shipping Pedors products from Chinese factories to U.S. warehouses, UPS pays the Chinese supplier up front for the goods. Pedors wires UPS half the cost of the shipment once the shoes leave China and has 60 days to pay the balance, with interest.

Pedors Chief Executive John O'Hare says working with UPS has helped his firm expand its product line. "This service cuts out all the middlemen in international trade," he says. Prior to the UPS deal, O'Hare relied on a bank credit line secured by his personal assets. With UPS, the collateral is the shipment itself. Your vendor can help you to reduce the cost of doing business.

Change is good. Change challenges companies to move beyond the business as usual mindset. Americans will come shining through this downturn as they change with the market change. Risks were taken, the economy went up in smoke, and now it's time to rise from the ashes.

The value analysis concept is a driver for change. Kodak (EK) could have made more money if it had grasped the threat of digital photography. As for IBM, it didn't take the personal computer seriously.

They had this vision of what a computer was and they never imagined anything different would take off. A competitive product must address factors such as cost, performance, aesthetics, schedule or time-to-market, and quality. The importance of these factors will vary from product to product and market to market. In addition, over time, users of a product will demand more and more performance at a lower cost.

Cost will become a more important factor in the acquisition of consumer products in two situations. First as the technology or aesthetics of a product matures or stabilizes the competitive playing field levels. Competition is increasingly the basis of cost or price.

Second, a customer's internal economics or financial resource limitations may shift the acquisition decision toward affordability as a more dominant factor. In either case, a successful product supplier must focus more attention on managing product cost.

Once the design of the product has been established, relatively little latitude exists to reduce the cost of a product. Decisions made after the product moves into production account for another ten to fifteen percent of the product's costs.

Similarly, decisions made about reducing existing general and administrative costs account for another ten to fifteen percent of the product's cost. When a company faces a profitability and cash flow crisis, this typically reduces research and development expenditures and lowers focus on post-development activities such as production enhancements.

The problem is that if cost containment is too little too late, business owners will experience higher unit costs and lower margins. This will lead to the company's inability to compete. A cost reduction program has to start with the design of the company's products at the very beginning of the development cycle.

In many companies, production cost considerations are an afterthought. The primary focus is on product performance or technology. Companies may get by with this approach in some markets and with some products in the short term, but ultimately the competition will catch up and the product will no longer be competitive.

Projected costs of production are estimates based on drawings and accumulated from quotes and manufacturing estimates. If these projected costs are too high relative to competitive conditions in a downward economy customers will reject the product. To remain competitive, the idea is to have low cost high value products.

Tweaking the effectiveness and cost of components using value analysis should occur before the product goes to production. This re-evaluation of processes and unit costs enables the business entity to maintain a competitive edge in a shrinking economy.

Cost Concept

A cost approach consists of the following elements:

- An understanding of customer affordability or competitive pricing requirements by the key participants in the development process
- Establishment and allocation of target costs down to a level where costs can be effectively managed
- Commitment by development personnel to development budgets and target costs
- Stability and management of requirements to balance requirements with affordability and to avoid creeping elegance
- An understanding of the product's cost drivers and consideration of cost drivers in establishing product specifications and in focusing attention on cost reduction
- Creative exploration of concept and design alternatives as a basis for developing lower cost design approaches
- Access to cost data to support this process and empower development team members
- Use of value analysis / function analysis and its derivatives (e.g., function analysis system technique) to understand essential product functions and to identify functions with a high cost to function ratio for further cost reduction
- Application of design for manufacturability principles as a key cost reduction tactic

- Meaningful cost accounting systems using cost techniques such as activity-based costing (ABC) to provide improved cost data
- Consistency of accounting methods between cost systems and product cost models as well as periodic validation of product cost models
- Continuous improvement through value engineering improves product value over the longer term

Kenneth Crow. http://www.npd-solutions.com/kcrow.html (accessed May 18, 2008).

What Is The Value Of A Burger Meal?

Fast food restaurants are testing smaller Hamburger Patties as they try to overcome high ingredient costs that are eating into profits. To combat costs patties are reduced to two ounces apiece from 2.2 ounces in some markets and there is continuing experimentations with different beverage sizes.

A quarter pound burger is no more a quarter pound.

Sales price for a Combo Meal - $4.59

Cost for the Combo Meal:
Double Cheeseburger: $.99
Medium Fries approximate count 55 fries: $.35
Medium Drink approximately 2 cents per ounce: $.32
Wrap, box and straw approximately: $.50
Approximate Total Cost $2.11
Approximate Margin: **$2.39**

Restaurants are in the business of making a profit. Times are hard; however, fast food joints have been able to increase their profits by increasing the price and reducing the quantity. In addition, they have the luxury of increasing sales volume in this shrinking economic environment because everybody has to eat. Therefore, it is more cost effective for consumers to get the whole family involved in cooking rather than eating out on a regular basis. In addition to that, you will be able to eat more than once.

Across the industry, restaurant chains are tweaking dishes or shrinking portions to save money. Shaving costs occur by selling food items with fewer ingredients.

Some pizza restaurants recently started using a lower-cost, high-moisture mozzarella (high in water and oil) that spreads better when it melts, leading to a reduction for cheese needed on each pizza.

Many food chains continue to reduce ingredient costs that make up the products that they sell. This helps to strengthen the bottom line.

Financial services organizations are also exercising their options to improve the bottom line. These options range from managing health-care costs, fishing out services and labor related redundancies, consolidating supplier relationships by geography or regions and by renegotiating contracts. Every business is into lean and providing low-cost high value to the customer, which is the bottom line.

22

A WORD FOR MAIN STREET

"I think it's going to last a lot longer than perhaps we would have anticipated." Anne Mulcahy, former chief executive of Xerox Corp. "This has been the worst financial crisis since the Great Depression. There is no question about it," said Mark Gertler, a New York University economist.

Moreover, to think, it was only a few months ago that wags such as myself were making light of people who had begun to compare the mortgage mess to the Great Depression.

On The Record

Should we still put our confidence in Wall Street? Wall Street rallies when the department of labor job claims report indicates an increase in unemployment. Corporate results that beat Wall Street's expectations through cost-cutting and government assistance is greeted by investors' cheers. **This is an indicator of how much Wall Street is out of touch with Main Street reality**.

Congress has moved more swiftly to approve fiscal stimulus than most thought possible. In part, the broader economy holds steady because exports have been so strong at just the right moment—a reminder of the global economy's importance to the U.S.

The market goes in waves and those who know about socionomics (mass psychology of crowds) know that market depressions happen once a century. The message is simple: "Get your financial house in order." The reality is that trickle-down stimulus to Main Street consumers is going to be slow and may not happen anytime soon. Do not pin your hopes and dreams on stimulus handouts. If your plan A is to wait on a stimulus, your plan B should be self preservation.

Everyone talks about the Great Depression of 1929-1933 but no one talks about the depression that happened during 1835-1842. This is the beginning of a depression and this has been coming for a while now (since the market topped in 2000).

Corporate-turnaround professionals and bankruptcy lawyers are either predicting a wave of retailer bankruptcies this year after being contacted by big and small retailers preparing to file for Chapter 11 bankruptcy protection or scrambling to avoid that fate.

Analysts estimate that 10% to 26% of all retailers are in financial distress and filing for Chapter 11 is inevitable. Alix Partners LLP, a Michigan-based turnaround-consulting firm, estimates that 25.8% of 182 large retailers it tracks are at significant risk of filing for bankruptcy or facing financial distress in 2009 or 2010.

As we continue the journey through this financial recovery, America and Americans are destined to thrive. Will you be ready for it?

FDIC Insurance

The Federal Deposit Insurance Corp. (FDIC) guarantees deposits up to $200,000 per person per deposit. If you have to hold more than that, spread it across multiple banks. As a taxpayer, you are paying for this insurance, so use it.

First, IRAs are covered by FDIC insurance up to $250,000 and it is possible to get more than $100,000 dollars in coverage for an individual account and more than $200,000 dollars in coverage for a joint account by utilizing beneficiaries or payable upon death designations.

For example, if John Doe has $1,000,000 dollars in a checking account and has his nine grandchildren on his account as beneficiaries, the account is not at risk by FDIC insurance standards, as each deposit has a $200,000 cover. The point is, speak with your bank representative if you have over 200,000 dollars deposited. There are ways to increase your insurance, and there is no need in some cases to have to keep up with multiple accounts around town because of fear of not having your money sufficiently covered by the FDIC.

www.thestreetratings.com is a good website to see the countries strongest and weakest banks.

Final Comment

I went to the local supermarket today and while shopping, there was a woman with her ten-year-old boy and his baby sister. The little boy struck me because he was clenching a bunch of coupons taken out of the local paper. The mother said to me that she is helping her son to understand the importance of being fiscally responsible. We have the power to raise a generation that will be either fiscally responsible or reckless. This crisis has given us an opportunity to be better examples and stewards for the next generation and beyond.

The speed at which global economies have declined in the last twelve months has caused shockwaves and is still causing aftershocks through the global community. The descent has caught consumers, countries and corporations by surprise.

The American consumer is disappointed not only at themselves for not paying attention to the level of personal excess and lack of savings but also at the financial system and how far unbridled risk-taking has gone off-track. Excess and bad money management replaced common sense. However, this current crisis is a wake-up call and presents a great opportunity to fix the problem which greed has perpetuated.

The long list of actions provided in this book is aimed at getting expenses aligned with your economic reality. The action taken today determines the strength of your recovery tomorrow.

The media promoted excess, then turned around and advocated restraint. There seems to be confusion and mixed messaging in respect to what communication is in the best interest of the American consumer.

During this economic crisis, fear replaced confidence—the fear of not knowing if your job is secure or whether you can hold on to your home for another month, another year. Fear has put a lock on consumer spending. Remember, fear is the enemy of hope. The night is quickly passing and daybreak is on the horizon. Hope has never been stronger in adversity.

The future calls for courage not retreat in adversity. There is no challenge high enough; there is no problem deep enough to prevent that true American spirit from coming through. Americans thrive on adversity; we evolve from struggles, to pass the greatest of tests that life throws our way. Courage is not only about taking risks, courage is standing tall when everything else shrinks around us. This is our time to rise up, shine and thrive.

Common sense is not so common! Everyone has it; not everyone chooses to exercise it. The baseline for common sense is being practical, following your gut, and making the best and prudent choice out of many. Common sense is the basis of instinct, insight and using your best judgment when presented with a range of choices.

If common sense were an article to be bought in the market, doubtless there would be a great demand for it, or if not, it would be well for the corporation to make an appropriation from the public money to buy up a lot, from which the needy might draw without any charge. http://query.nytimes.com (accessed January 18, 2007).

Common sense is the counter-balance that helps us to use sound and practical judgment. It enables us to manage our money confidently and secure our families' future. When your judgment is challenged in a time of crisis, view your challenges and mistakes as a life experience, Embrace the experience, move beyond it and thrive!

"When one door of happiness closes, another opens; but often we look so long at the closed door that we do not see the one which has been opened for us."
Helen Keller. http://www.beyondthequote.com/helen-keller-quotes.html (accessed September 1, 2009).

Some men give up their designs when they have almost reached the goal;

While others, on the contrary, obtain a victory by exerting, at the last moment, most vigorous efforts than before.

Polybius
Greek statesman & historian
c.120bc

GLOSSARY OF TERMS

Aftershock - A further reaction following the shock of a deeply disturbing occurrence or revelation: "The industry continued to reel from aftershocks of a disastrous [year]"

APR - The yearly cost of a mortgage, including interest, mortgage insurance, and the origination fee (points), expressed as a percentage. The annual percentage rate can be looked at in two primary ways: the nominal rate, which is a non-adjusted simple interest rate, or the effective rate, which takes compound interest into account

Budget - A systematic plan for the expenditure of a usually fixed resource, such as money or time, during a given period

Calibrate - alter or regulate so as to achieve accuracy or conform to a standard

Common sense - sound practical judgment

Compound interest - arises when interest is added to the principal, so that from that moment on, the interest that has been added *also itself* earns interest. This addition of interest to the principal is called *compounding* (i.e. the interest is compounded). A loan, for example, may have its interest compounded every month: in this case, a loan with $100 initial principal and 1% interest per month would have a balance of $101 at the end of the first month, $102.01 at the end of the second month, and so on

Consignment - When goods are delivered to another company with the understanding that payment for the goods is only made once the goods are sold

Consumer - A consumer is someone who can make the decision whether or not to purchase an item at the store, and someone who can be influenced by marketing and advertisements

Deferred - Suspended or withheld for or until a certain time or

Delinquent - An account, tax, debt, etc. past due; overdue

Disposable Income – Is the after-tax income that is calculated quarterly which consumers have available for spending or saving. Economists view changes in disposable income as an important indicator of the present and future health of the economy

Earned Income Credit - Earned Income Tax Credit is a benefit to help low-income workers by offsetting part of their Social Security and Medicare taxes

Empowerment - To equip or supply with ability; enable

Haggling - To cut (something) in a crude, unskillful manner; hack.

Inaction - Lack or absence of action

Layaway - event: a deferred payment; deferred taxes
A payment plan in which a buyer reserves an article of merchandise by placing a deposit with the retailer until the balance is paid in full: *bought a suit on layaway*

Negotiation - mutual discussion and arrangement of the terms of a transaction or agreement

Nest egg - money saved and held in reserve for emergencies, retirement, etc

Overdraft - An overdraft occurs when withdrawals from a bank account exceed the available balance which gives the account a negative balance - a person can be said to be "overdrawn"

Perspective - A mental view or outlook

Prime - The group or borrowers deemed to be the most credit-worthy, indicated by a FICO score greater than 620. Prime borrowers are qualified to borrow at the market interest rate

Refinance - Is the process of paying off an existing loan by taking a new loan and using the same property as security

Homeowners may refinance to reduce their mortgage expense if interest rates have dropped, to switch from an adjustable to a fixed rate loan if rates are rising, or to draw on the equity that has built up during a period of rising home prices

Closing costs for a refinance are generally comparable to those for any mortgage. If you're refinancing to reduce your payments, you'll want to calculate how long it will take before you recover the closing costs and begin to save money

If you're planning to move within a few years, refinancing may not actually save you enough to justify the closing expenses. And if you refinance to use some of your home equity, you run the added risk that prices could drop and you could end up owing more on your mortgage than you could realize from selling your home

Simple Interest - The interest calculated on a principal sum, not compounded on earned interest

Socionomics - The Science of History and Social Prediction

Special Enrollment Period (SEP) - The new special enrollment rights are applicable to group health plans as defined under HIPAA, with the exception of health care flexible spending account arrangements

It is important to note that the new 60-day special enrollment period differs from the current HIPAA portability rule, which states an employee must generally be given at least *30 days* to request coverage under the employer's group health plan in the event of loss of other coverage or acquisition of a new dependent. And while IRC Section 125 regulations impose no maximum time period when requesting a mid-year election change, many plans are written to include 30-day notice periods to reflect the prior HIPAA special enrollment rights

Subprime - also called B-paper, near-prime, or second chance lending, is the practice of making loans to borrowers who do not qualify for the best market interest rates because of their deficient credit history. The term also refers to paper taken on property that cannot be sold on the primary market, including loans on certain types of investment properties and certain types of self-employed individuals. Subprime lending is risky for both lenders and borrowers due to the combination of high interest rates, poor credit history, and adverse financial situations usually associated with subprime applicants. A subprime loan is offered at a rate higher than A-paper loans due to the increased risk

Telematics - The integrated use of telecommunications and informatics, also known as ICT (Information and Communications Technology). More specifically it is the science of sending, receiving and storing information via telecommunication devices

The Great Depression - was a severe worldwide economic depression in the decade preceding World War II. The timing of the Great Depression varied across nations, but in most countries it started in about 1929 and lasted until the late 1930s or early 1940s. It was the longest, most widespread, and deepest depression of the 20th century, and is used

Thrive - To make steady progress; prosper

Unemployment - occurs when a person is available to work and seeking work but currently without work

Warranty - A guarantee given to the purchaser by a company stating that a product is reliable and free from known defects and that the seller will, without charge, repair or replace defective parts within a given time limit and under certain conditions

Acknowledgements and vote of thanks

Patricia and Aaron Ambersley
Professor Charles L. Meadows Ph.D.
Angela Woods
O'Neil Reid CPA
James Taylor Jr.
Kristen Faust
Jim Pierce
Mary Morris

Made in the USA
Charleston, SC
09 March 2010